What the Writing Tutor Needs to Know

Margot Iris Soven

La Salle University

THOMSON

WADSWORTH

Australia • Brazil • Canada • Mexico • Singapore
Spain • United Kingdom • United States

THOMSON

WADSWORTH

Publisher: *Michael Rosenberg*
Acquisitions Editor: *Dickson Musslewhite*
Development Editor: *Cheryl Forman*
Editorial Assistant: *Jonelle Lonergan*
Marketing Assistant: *Dawn Giovanniello*
Advertising Project Manager: *Patrick Rooney*

Editorial Production Manager: *Michael Burggren*
Manufacturing Supervisor: *Marcia Locke*
Cover Designer: *Dutton & Sherman Design*
Production Service/Compositor: *Integra*
Cover/Text Printer: *Malloy Incorporated*

For more information about our products, contact us at:
Thomson Learning Academic Resource Center
1-800-423-0563

For permission to use material from this text or product, submit a request online at
http://www.thomsonrights.com.
Any additional questions about permissions can be submitted by email to
thomsonrights@thomson.com.

Library of Congress Control Number:
2005929904

ISBN 1-4130-0224-2

Thomson Higher Education
25 Thomson Place
Boston, MA 02210-1202
USA

Asia (including India)
Thomson Learning
5 Shenton Way
#01-01 UIC Building
Singapore 068808

Australia/New Zealand
Thomson Learning Australia
102 Dodds Street
Southbank, Victoria 3006
Australia

Canada
Thomson Nelson
1120 Birchmount Road
Toronto, Ontario M1K 5G4
Canada

UK/Europe/Middle East/Africa
Thomson Learning
High Holborn House
50/51 Bedford Row
London WC1R 4LR
United Kingdom

Latin America
Thomson Learning
Seneca, 53
Colonia Polanco
11560 Mexio
D.F. Mexico

Spain (includes Portugal)
Thomson Paraninfo
Calle Magallanes, 25
28015 Madrid, Spain

Contents

Preface

On a hot July afternoon in the summer of 1986, a conversation took place in the La Salle University faculty dining room that would eventually lead to the transformation of our writing across the curriculum program. Having just returned from a writing across the curriculum conference at SUNY Farmingdale, two of my colleagues, one in biology, and one in economics, were eager to discuss Tori Haring Smith's presentation about the Writing Fellows Program, a peer tutoring program, at Brown University. They were more than enthusiastic about Brown's key technique of assigning peer tutors, called Writing Fellows, to classes in all disciplines with substantial writing requirements, and were eager to start a similar program at La Salle. After a trip to Brown University and further discussions with Dr. Haring Smith, we were convinced: writing tutors attached to specific classes seemed like an idea worth trying. La Salle was already using writing tutors in our writing center with impressive success.

Up until that time faculty development had been the centerpiece of our writing across the curriculum program. Now, 17 years later (Time flies when you are having fun!), peer tutoring not only augments faculty development in the area of writing instruction, but adds a much valued student-centered dimension to teaching writing.

We are by no means unique. The number of Writing Fellows programs continues to grow. Of course, writing centers have long existed at large state universities, small liberal arts colleges, two-year colleges, and Ivy League schools. Peer tutoring is recognized as a powerful educational tool, not only in writing, but in all subjects. Why is this the case? Kenneth Bruffee says it best: "Peer tutors as a group, acting collaboratively, are potentially the most powerful agents for educational change, because peer tutors learn the most important tool for effecting change, the art of translation—the art of conversation at the boundaries between communities." In other words, not only do peer tutors help students transition into the academic community by helping them with their writing but they also help faculty to better understand "where their students are coming from," which in turn leads to better writing assignments and instruction which is student centered.

During my 20-plus years in higher education, I have worn several administrative hats: "Composition Program Director," "Writing Across the Curriculum Coordinator," and, as I write this book, "Core Curriculum Director," and "Writing Fellows Program Director." Each of these positions has presented challenges and offered immense rewards. However, as I think back, the position that has provided the most satisfaction to me as a teacher is my directorship of the Writing Fellows program. The wide-ranging effects of writing tutors that Bruffee describes never cease to impress me.

If you are reading this book, you are in training to become a peer tutor in your school's writing center or Writing Fellows program. You will not only help your fellow students, but, believe it or not, you will change the way your instructors assign and evaluate writing. You will increase your knowledge about writing, and the nature of higher education, and you will get to know many students you would never have met if you had not become a peer tutor. You are about to participate in what will be one of the most valuable educational experiences your college has to offer.

Acknowledgments

My career in education has taken many interesting turns. Along the way I have had the good fortune to meet up with many educators who were interested in new ideas. In the 1970s I "crossed over" from a doctoral program in American literature to a doctoral program in the Teaching of Writing. This would not have been possible without Norma Kahn, my thesis advisor in the Graduate School of Education at the University of Pennsylvania.

Lucky for me, I then landed at La Salle University, a school where dedication to teaching is not limited to flowery statements in the College Bulletin. My colleagues, both faculty and administrators, encourage innovative programs, such as the Writing Fellows Program, and continue to support programs which improve learning. I am grateful to them, especially John Keenan and James Butler, former English Department Chairs, Kevin Harty, current Chair of the English Department, Br. Emery Mollenhauer, former Provost, and Richard Nigro, current Provost of La Salle University, for their support in the past and the present.

I also thank my children, Josh, Andy, Ruthy, and my mom and dad, Esther and Paul Korman, my greatest cheerleaders, along with my brothers, Ira and Roger, and my sisters-in-law, Sara and Fanny, whose love and sense of humor are such an important part of my life.

As always, I am grateful for my husband Paul's encouragement, sound advice, and patience with yet another writing project!

Margot Soven
La Salle University

Introduction

To the Instructor

When I first started training peer tutors in the mid-1980s, most of the training models were based on the assumption that the tutors would be working in writing centers and training would take place over the period of a week, if that long. Training materials concentrated on methods for conducting successful conferences (for example Harris, Reigstad, and McAndrew). However, coincident with the emergence of Writing Fellow programs, where tutors (student "peers") are assigned to specific courses to work with all of the students in a specific course, training programs became more extensive. I have some theories as to why the weeklong training period evolved into a course.

- More prestige. The status of writing tutors changed. Being assigned to courses gave writing tutors more prestige. They were now called "Writing Fellows" and "Writing Associates."
- Closer connection to the faculty. Directors of Writing Fellows programs became more concerned about the quality of training, now that writing tutors were working directly with faculty.
- The emergence of "writing across the curriculum" programs. The WAC movement had a great impact on tutor preparation. The idea that academic writing was more than a generic skill, but had something to do with knowledge of particular forms of writing in different disciplines made us realize that we needed to add a new component to the peer tutor's training. Tutors had to become acquainted with discourse theory, at least as it pertained to academic writing. Thus the semester-long course for training peer tutors was implemented at many schools.

The training of writing tutors who staff writing centers also began to change to incorporate study of the forms of writing used in the various academic disciplines. Although many of these training programs are still limited to a single week, they are no longer restricted to only reviewing methods of conducting writing conferences.

Keep in mind that as with most issues in the academic world, the best plan for training writing tutors is not a subject about which those of us who direct training programs agree. Some courses or workshops resemble advanced writing courses (for example, the University of Pennsylvania, Pennsylvania State University) where the students simulate the peer tutoring situation by critiquing each other's drafts. In these courses, students do study theory related to peer tutoring, but the main activities in the course are writing and reviewing each other's papers. These courses are typically offered in English Departments. They are based on the idea that to become a good tutor you need to identify with the students you will tutor by becoming more aware of what it feels like to write and to have your writing critiqued by a peer. Of course, you also gain experience as a peer tutor when you critique your classmate's work.

Other courses are modeled on the one developed by Tori-Haring Smith at Brown University. The underlying rationale for this group of courses is that peer tutors should become reflective practitioners. They should be able to evaluate their performance as a peer tutor and continue to improve. The best way for them to achieve this goal is to compare their experiences as a peer tutor to the theory and research in the field. These courses often require students to read about topics related to peer tutoring and, in addition, to practice strategies recommended for conferencing and writing comments. Often students are required to conduct research projects related to the tutoring situations at their own universities. For example, students might interview faculty to learn about their criteria for evaluating student papers.

How This Book Is Constructed

This book follows the organization of a course, *Writing and the University*, that I teach for peer tutors at La Salle University. Our course is based on the philosophy of training peer tutors originally developed at Brown University. When I first began teaching it the students were required to read a great deal about research and theory in composition. However, after several years of tepid student evaluations I began to get the message: Theory was important, but the students wanted more class time to discuss and practice their peer-tutoring skills. I learned that students enter peer-tutoring programs because they want to become peer tutors, not because they have a burning interest in composition theory. As with any course, mine is situated somewhere between what the instructor thinks the student needs to know and what the student wants to know!

This book can be used for short workshops as well as for full-length courses. Each chapter is basically self-contained, but occasionally contains references to related material in other chapters. Chapters 2, 3, and 4 summarize the basics of peer tutoring. The information in the text comes from a variety of sources: experts in the field, my colleagues, my own observations and experience, and, most important, the observations and research of writing tutors at La Salle.

Using the exercises at the end of each chapter, students can practice (and question) the techniques presented in this book. Furthermore, by including examples from the experience and research of many writing tutors I hope to send a strong message to future writing tutors: they can become reflective practitioners by conducting their own research, even as they embark on their first tutoring experiences.

A Word About Instructors Writing Assignments and Student Papers in the Book

I have included two types of materials:

1. Sample assignments which appear exactly as they were presented to the students, with the permission of the faculty who contributed them for the book.
2. "Student" papers that were actually written by me, except for one case where I have permission from the student to use her paper. I constructed the sample papers using actual student papers as models or archetypes of various kinds of student essays.

To the Student with Peer-Tutoring Jitters

Students in my peer tutor-training course are sometimes quite apprehensive about the whole enterprise. I ask them how they feel about peer tutoring and invariably some say, "I'm afraid I won't be able to help anyone. [...] Maybe I won't be able to recognize all of their mistakes [...] Why should my fellow students take my advice? After all, I'm only a student myself [...] What if the student I help receives a poor grade, even after

I give him some suggestions? [...] What if the student's teacher thinks I gave her incorrect advice?"

Patricia Dolnick, a peer tutor at La Salle, describes her apprehensions about peer tutoring, and how, by the end of the semester, she had conquered them.

> With almost everything I do for the first time, I tend to start off with some uncertainty clouding my mind. Deciding to become a writing tutor was not an exception, as I have felt much uncertainty weighing me down throughout the start of the semester. I was apprehensive that I would not be able to do a good job helping students revise their papers. Being the only Finance major amidst a classroom of English, Psychology, and Communication majors, I was afraid that I wouldn't have the same level of writing skills they possess. As we practiced revising sample papers and doing mock conferences, my fears started to subside, but I was still afraid to have a tutee put faith in my suggestions. There have been times in class when I sat and wondered if I really should be a writing tutor, but after the first semester I am feeling more and more confident in myself. "Round one" has really opened my eyes to what the writing process is and how to break it down for others. I was pleasantly surprised to find the students very relaxed during their conferences and extremely friendly. The first round of tutoring has proved to be a great learning experience in helping others and in creating a unique opportunity to test my own writing skills.

Perhaps you too are somewhat anxious, as you begin a peer-tutoring training program. Patricia's experience should be an inspiration!

Here are some words of wisdom (based on nearly 20 years of training peer tutors and directing a peer-tutoring program) I share with my peer tutors:

- Tutoring writing is not brain surgery; no one dies if you miss a comma error.
- You can help students with their writing. Theory and research related to the effects of peer tutoring is very positive. We'll review these theories and some of the research in Chapter 1.
- Most students are grateful for the writing tutors' help. Although they may appear skeptical when it is suggested that they need help with their writing and should visit the writing center, student surveys indicate that most students believe that writing tutors give them good advice.

- Most instructors give high praise to the performance of writing tutors. Instructors who send students to writing centers are pleased with the results. The same is true for faculty who participate in Writing Fellows programs. I've been told that "The Writing Fellows program is one of the best programs in the school. Keep up the good work!"
- Take some of the pressure off yourself when you first begin to work with students by reminding them that you are not an expert—that you give your suggestions from your perspective as a good student writer. They can take your advice or not, as they see fit. The paper is still their responsibility, not yours.
- Grades are none of your business. You are not a teacher-clone or teacher-substitute. The instructor gives the grade.

And, perhaps most important of all, remember that having been chosen to be a writing tutor means that *you* are a good writer. You already know a great deal about writing, and more than likely a great deal about peer tutoring as well. Like many of the students in my class, you probably have been helping your friends with their papers for years. The major difference, as some of my students say, is that now they are getting paid!

How Can This Book Help You to Become an Effective Writing Tutor?

This book covers the material you should know to become an effective tutor:

- Why peer tutoring works.
- How peer tutors differ from teachers.
- Why many students have problems with academic writing.
- How to conduct student–tutor conferences.
- How to respond in writing to drafts.
- How to help students whose papers exhibit a variety of problems.
- How to work with different kinds of students: the basic writer, the very good writer, the average writer, the ESL student, the adult student, and the student with writing anxiety.
- Teacher expectations.
- Tutoring online.

Here is a synopsis of each chapter:

Chapter 1: Peer Tutoring and College Writing: Peer Tutoring Works!

The tutor in the writing center taught me how to revise.

This chapter draws on theory and research that demonstrates the value of peer tutoring for meeting the specific goals of college writing instruction. Most scholars in the field agree that the ability to write an essay generally free from error is only one of these goals and not even the most important. Peer tutoring can help students increase competency in several areas: understanding the writing process, knowledge of the rhetorical conventions of academic discourse in a variety of disciplines, and the acquisition of a vocabulary for talking about writing. Research on peer response groups, research on conferences, and analyses of the nature of academic discourse will be integrated into this discussion.

Chapter 2: Where We Tutor—How We Tutor

I have no idea how to begin.

The chapter includes an explanation of the special characteristics of various tutoring "sites" and a brief history of writing centers and Writing Fellows Programs. You will learn the basic principles of peer tutoring that apply in just about all peer tutoring situations.

Chapter 3: How to Conference and Write Comments

The written comments were to help me revise, but in the conference I could ask for a further explanation.

This chapter introduces you to the special language of peer tutoring and some of the practical issues involved in conferencing and writing comments. It covers very basic topics such as scheduling, the length of conferences and the logistics of receiving and returning papers. It also includes suggestions for actively involving the student in the revision process. Several modes of response, related to the different contexts in which the tutors read papers, will be discussed. For example, the tutor in a drop-in writing center must know how to read and respond without seeing the paper beforehand. The tutor in curriculum-based peer tutoring programs (commonly called Writing Fellows programs) will often read the paper and write comments prior to meeting the student at a short conference. Examples of tutors' responses to papers will be included.

Chapter 4: Common Writing Problems: Focus, Organization, Development, Style, and Correctness

Please say my draft is good!

The focus of this chapter is a series of papers exemplifying problems typical of many first drafts: ideas are insufficiently developed and/or not organized logically and the papers lack focus and/or exhibit sentence level problems. The drafts will come from courses in several disciplines. Strategies for identifying the problems and for responding to them through written comments or in conferences will form the content of most of this chapter.

Chapter 5: The Writing Process of College Students

Do I really need to revise?

This chapter is very down to earth. I not only review seminal articles on the composing process, such as those by Linda Flower and Nancy Sommers, but also refer to the more recent studies by Linda Cleary on the relationship between motivation and student writing. Special attention is paid to the revision stage of writing, where writing tutors often have the most impact.

Chapter 6: Tutoring Special Students

I'm a nurse; this is my first college course in twenty years!

Nontraditional students—adult learners, ESL students, students with learning difficulties—form a major portion of the population at many colleges. Many of the tutoring techniques discussed in earlier chapters can be used successfully with these students. However, the tutor must also be prepared to deal with issues unrelated to writing competence, such as the anxiety that often accompanies being different. Also, the tutor must be prepared to make adjustments in format, such as conferencing on the phone rather than meeting on campus. Online tutoring, especially for adult learners, might also be effective. This chapter will discuss the special needs of these students and suggest strategies for meeting them.

Chapter 7: Teacher Expectations, Writing Assignments, and Peer Tutoring: What's the Connection?

> I have a twenty-page research paper due in my freshman history class! I wonder if my teacher takes off for commas.

Fact or fiction? "Writing assignments in different disciplines are different." This chapter demonstrates that simple categorizations of writing assignments are mostly false. In fact there is some research which indicates that writing assignments in introductory courses in many disciplines are remarkably similar. However, the chapter also reveals that there is considerable variation in teachers' expectations in terms of style, format, and in their tolerance for error. Some of these differences are related to disciplinary differences; others are not. Excerpts from teacher interviews conducted by tutors are included in this chapter.

Chapter 8: Tutoring Online: An Option— But Is It a Good One?

> Dear tutor, Can I email my draft to you tonight? I can have it to you by 3 am. By the way, it's due for my 9:00 class. Please advise. Thanks much!

The electronic world beckons. We've all heard stories about students who would prefer to remain "online" except perhaps for the weekend fraternity party. Online courses are increasingly popular—even in composition. The advantages are many: immediate access, no problem finding the writing center, and so on. But there are disadvantages as well. Is it possible to be a "coach" online? Is something lost as we try to "interface with the face-less?" I discuss the pros and cons of online tutoring from the perspective of students and tutors who have experimented with it. I also include a description of online resources for students and instructors. Some of these resources are especially useful for tutors.

Works Cited

Cleary, Linda Miller. *From the Other Side of the Desk. Students Speak About Writing*. Portsmouth, NH: Heinemann Boynton/Cook, 1991.

Flower, Linda. "Writer Based Prose: A Cognitive Basis for Problems in Writing." *College English*. 41 (September 1979): 19–37.

Harris, Muriel. *Teaching One on One: The Writing Conference*. Urbana, IL: NCTE, 1986.

Reigstad, Thomas J. and Donald McAndrew. *Training Tutors for Writing Conferences*. Urbana, IL: NCTE, 1984.

Sommers, Nancy. "Revision and Student Writers and Experienced Adult Writers." *The Writing Teachers Sourcebook*. 2nd ed. Ed. Gary Tate and Edward Corbett. New York: Oxford University Press, 1988.

1

Peer Tutoring and College Writing: Peer Tutoring Works!

Collaborative learning is "an old principle which wise teachers have known for ages—that students can teach each other things which resist assimilation through the direct instruction of a teacher."

—Kenneth Bruffee "Peer Tutoring and the Conversation of Mankind"

What you do as a tutor, as I understand it is to help a tutee cross the boundary between one knowledge community and another. You do that by helping the tutee learn about the new community. Knowledge communities, or if you prefer, discourse communities, are groups of people who talk the same way. The boundaries between knowledge communities are defined by the words, turns of phrases, and styles of speaking that writing communities agree on as they construct the knowledge that is their common property.

—Kenneth Bruffee "Lost in Translation: Peer Tutors, Faculty Members, and the Art of Boundary Conversation"

Conferences, opportunities for highly productive dialogues between writers and teacher-readers, are and should be an integral part of teaching writing. It is in the one-to-one setting of a conference that we can meet with writers and hear them talk about their writing. And they can hear us talk, not about writing in the abstract, but about their writing. This conversation should not be viewed as merely an adjunct to group instruction, for some of the more vocal advocates of writing conferences consider the conference to be the prime method of writing for teaching writing.

—Muriel Harris *Teaching One to One*

Kenneth Bruffee and Muriel Harris, two names you will get to know if you are a writing tutor in training, tell us that peer tutoring is a form of collaborative learning that can play an important role in the teaching of writing, and that conferencing is a crucial part of the process. Here are some reasons that peer tutoring in writing is extremely effective:

1. Peer tutors have the advantage of being in the same social and academic situation as the students they tutor. Instructors get only a glimpse of what it's like to juggle the conflicting demands of the college years. Whether you are a commuter or live on your college campus, you know what I mean. When instructors see a poor paper, they usually don't think to themselves, "Hmm—was this student having a bad week? Maybe she had an argument with her boyfriend, or had to work late at her job off campus." *Coming of Age in New Jersey* by Michael Moffatt, one of the most revealing discussions about campus life outside the classroom, should be required reading, not for you, but for your instructors. Moffatt, an anthropologist at Rutgers University in New Jersey, found that although students considered academics important, much of their time at college they were preoccupied with social concerns.

2. Peer tutors can better sympathize with students' writing problems. Although peer tutors are good writers, they, like the students they tutor, are often unsure about how to tackle one of our "creative" writing assignments. They too have been overwhelmed by having to write several papers in the week. Instructors may not realize that often their writing assignment is faulty or that their students have multiple writing assignments due on the same day.

3. Peer tutors often have more time than faculty do to help students with their writing. Anyone who has volunteered to be a writing tutor has scheduled time for just that purpose. Instructors often want to read drafts, but when they are teaching four courses, as we do at La Salle, that may be impossible.

4. Peer tutors do not give grades. Learning to write can be inhibited by the specter of a grade. Maureen Cech, one of our peer tutors at La Salle reported, after interviewing a student about his attitudes towards peer tutoring: "Richard feels that a student's comments are especially helpful, since (ironically) they don't hold the weight of an instructor's comments. He knows that when I read his papers, I am not going to grade them. He believes that I am there to help him improve his current paper, as well as to help him write better papers in the future; and while he does know that ultimately a teacher has the same purpose, a teacher's evaluation holds a much more dreaded consequence—the grade!"

Some composition scholars take issue with the idea that good student writers can be regarded as peers of their tutees. For example, Irene Clark and David Healy assert that "many tutors are not peers in any sense of the word." They argue that tutors are chosen because they have demonstrated an ability to write which automatically eliminates their peer status, because those commonly seeking help at a writing center are those who have demonstrated an inability to write—at least to write well (33). However, most experts argue that the tutor's peer status on other levels is what opens the possibility that well-trained tutors can actually help their clients become better writers, not just people in possession of better texts.

As with other innovations in the teaching of writing, we owe the popularization of peer tutoring to particular individuals, in this case Kenneth Bruffee (Brooklyn College) and Muriel Harris (Purdue University). Bruffee is the undisputed theoretical guru of collaborative learning and peer tutoring and an important spokesperson for the social constructionist (see p. 10) view of the development of writing ability. Muriel Harris deserves credit for research on the writing conference and for her aggressive promotion of conferencing as an important supplement to the classroom approach to teaching of writing. These two lines of inquiry and practice came together at just the moment when large numbers of underprepared students were given access to the City University in New York in the late 1960s, and writing centers or Learning Centers were established to meet the growing need for remediation. (See Chapter 2 for a more detailed discussion about the history of writing centers.)

Open enrollment, an admissions policy in which underprepared students were admitted to the City University of New York, may have been the catalyst for the growth of tutoring in writing, but it was also common sense that drove the peer-tutoring revolution. Kenneth Bruffee makes this point most cogently in his landmark essay "Peer Tutoring and the Conversation of Mankind." He says that there were several common denominators that characterized many students who did not do well in college in the 1960s: they had difficulty adapting to the traditional conventions of the college classroom and refused professional help when it was offered. Some instructors decided that an alternative to the traditional classroom might be a more effective way of addressing these students' needs. Enter peer tutoring, "which did not change what students learned, but, rather the social context in which they learned it" (4). Furthermore, peer tutoring was an attractive solution to the problem of poor writing because peer tutoring was *reciprocal*—both the tutee and the tutor benefited. Bruffee points out that the review of research (which already supported the value of peer tutoring) and the evolution of a theoretical rationale supporting peer tutoring came later (5).

In the remainder of this chapter, I present a brief summary of several different theories which explain why tutoring works in the context of composition theory and review some of the research which confirms the value of peer tutoring. The terms *theory* and *research* can be somewhat daunting. You might ask, "Why do I need to know about theory and research? How can theory help me become a better writing tutor?" The way I see it, theory and research strengthen one's commitment to accepted practices and encourage a positive attitude to self-sponsored research and discovery. If, for example, your first efforts at tutoring writing do not go well, you will have theory and research results to fall back on. You will be less likely to become discouraged if at first you don't succeed. Also, because theory helps you understand the basis for practice, you are then able to seek alternative theories and practices if you are experienced and can evaluate your methods. Becoming a practitioner in any field takes time and practice; it involves trial and error. Theory and research support the new practitioner during this process and remind the seasoned practitioner to continue to question what he does.

I believe that modern theory and research debunk the idea that peer tutoring is one of those educational fads that will have its day, only to be replaced by yet another educational fad. Most peer-tutoring programs, whether, they occur in writing centers or are curriculum based (for example Writing Fellows programs), should no longer be viewed as a supplement to conventional writing instruction. The substantial literature on both theory and research confirm the value of peer tutoring in writing as an integral part of teaching writing.

Peer-Tutoring Theory in Context: The "Teaching Writing" Revolution

The theories which support peer tutoring are firmly grounded in the theories and research which led to the revolution in teaching writing. My teaching career is a microcosm of this revolution. As a college student in the 1960s majoring in English Education my preparation to teach writing consisted of the study of two texts: *Teaching English Grammar* and *Teaching English Usage*, both by Robert Pooley. In my first teaching job in a small private school in Chicago, the writing part of the curriculum consisted of pointing out grammar and usage errors in my students' essays and teaching them how to correct them. Fortunately I was teaching good students who were able to do what I had done as a student: figure out how to write through trial and error.

After moving back east and spending several years at home raising a family, I returned to teaching writing in the mid-1970s as an adjunct at Drexel University. The composition faculty at Drexel was using two texts: *Telling Writing* by Ken Macrorie and *Writing Without Teachers* by Peter Elbow. Both of these texts focus on students rather than on the written product. Macrorie's book urges students to write about subjects of interest to them and not to worry, at least in the initial stages of writing, about correctness. Elbow's book stresses the importance of writing as a process and the value of students reading each other's work. The revolution in the teaching of writing was in full swing. Where did this new pedagogy come from? Why now? I returned to graduate school to find out.

Educational change never occurs in a straight line representing cause and effect. It would be nice and neat if I could tell you that public concern about teaching writing in the 1970s led to new theories which led to new practices. But educational change is never that simple. The revolution in teaching composition was influenced not only by the perception that students couldn't write but also by the political movements in the 1960s (for example women's liberation, the civil rights movement, the peace movement), which despite their differences had a similar aim—to liberate the individual from societal constraints and stereotypes: "Be yourself, Don't worry about convention" became the rallying cry of the 1960s.

At this time, students as opposed to content became the focus of educational reform. And once that happened, educators sought new methods for teaching students how to express themselves, since self-expression led to "being yourself." At the same time, educators also sought to revamp teaching methods by finding out more about how students learn. The teaching of writing was influenced by both of these objectives and underwent a transformation that is justifiably called a revolution.

The scope of this text does not permit a discussion of all the theoretical strands which formed the backdrop for this revolution, so I will focus on theories most related to the increased interest in peer tutoring as a method for improving writing: those supporting individualizing education and the importance of self-expression, and two alternative theories explaining how students learn to write, namely social theories based on cognitive psychology and those derived from social constructionist view.

Individualizing Education

The importance of individualizing instruction led to a paradigmatic shift in education on all fronts, not just the teaching of writing. On the elementary and secondary level, teachers seeking methods for individualizing education looked toward their counterparts in Great Britain for direction. In the early 1970s, the "open classroom," where students worked individually or in groups at their own speed and in their own way, became popular. We moved to Merion, a suburb of Philadelphia, in order for our children to attend an open classroom school. Writing was central to the open classroom. At the Merion School, third graders traveled from "learning station," to "learning station," clipboards in hand, recording their observations and ideas. On the college level, collaborative learning and one-on-one tutoring emerged as strategies for accomplishing similar aims. The theoretical support for these pedagogical shifts was found in the works of Carl Rogers and Benjamin Bloom among others. For example, in *Training Tutors for Writing Conferences* Reigstad and McAndrew (1984) cite Rogers and Bloom when they argue that one-to-one teaching is the ideal because this method focuses on the student: "The tutor's goal is to first discover what the student knows and needs to know; the tutor then tries to cue the student about what needs to be done, either by talking or demonstrating." Although the tutor knows the answers, the tutor tries to actively involve the student in the learning process (2).

Expressivism

Individualized instruction required more than paying attention to the different rate at which students learn and their different learning styles and abilities. The 1966 Dartmouth Conference, which took place at Dartmouth College, New Hampshire and which drew together 50 teachers from Great Britain and the United States, focused exclusively on English Education. The conference was a major force for changing the objectives and methodologies of English Education. As I pointed out in *Teaching Writing in Middle and Secondary Schools*, "participants agreed that increasing children's perception and self-awareness should be major objectives for language arts education [...]" Among their conclusions they agreed that "from the very start of [teaching] reading and writing. [the teacher] has to look beyond the minimum possibilities of literacy to the profounder possibilities of a considered and extended exploration of experience, permitting slower realizations and more individual growth" (Dixon 112). The participants agreed that writing should play a major role in freeing students to express their own ideas. Support for this goal came from other quarters as well. Rhetoricians such as James Kinneavy lamented the lack of attention to personal writing at all levels, pointing out that students should be taught how to write the personal essay to increase self-understanding (Kinneavy).

Where does peer tutoring fit in? Those who favor what came to be know as expressivisim as a basis for teaching writing believe that working with a peer tutor helps the writer retrieve the knowledge that the writer already possesses. Although a tutor tells the students what needs to be done, the tutor takes his or her cues from the students themselves, who presumably know more about the content of the paper than the tutor, but need some help retrieving that knowledge. John and Tilly Warnock, among others (for example Brannon and Knoblauch), believe that peer tutoring should "champion the writer's authority to speak and think, in contrast to the classroom where students are viewed as the ones who do not know" (20). Furthermore, the philosophy of some tutoring programs such as the one at Brown University emphasize "the students' right to their own text," a phrase coined by Brannon and

Knoblauch. The tutors in these programs are instructed to question students about their goals for the paper and help them achieve those goals. These programs strongly object to the view of the tutor as the instructor's messenger whose main job is to make sure that the tutee fulfills the requirements of the instructors' writing assignments.

How Students Learn to Write

In contrast to those educators whose main concern was individualizing instruction and using writing as a vehicle for self-awareness, another group of educators, who used cognitive psychology as a basis for their theories and research, focused on the act of writing itself. They theorized that if we knew more about what students were thinking about when they tried to accomplish a writing task, how they go about writing, and we compared the writing process of novice writers with the practices of experienced writers, we could transform the novice writers into experienced writers. Janet Emig (1971) found that novice writers truncated the writing process; they gave very little time to planning or revising. Her results were confirmed in Nancy Sommers' "Revision Strategies of Student Writers And Experienced Writers" (1988). They, along with Flowers and Hayes, found that experienced writers break down the writing process into planning, drafting, and revising stages. These stages are not necessarily discrete; they often overlap one another. For example, after an experienced writer has made some notes, planned her essay, and is in the middle of drafting it, she might discover that she lacks information on a part of the subject and must return to the note-taking stage. Or after the writer has completed a first draft and rereads it, she might decide to reorganize the information in the essay, which requires returning to the planning stage again. This theory guided the largest number of studies on teaching composition in the 1960s when the "Johnny Can't Write" alarms were first sounded. Through "think aloud" protocols (students actually speak out loud while they are writing) Linda Flower demonstrated that writing makes great demands on beginning writers who often experience "cognitive overload." The cognitivists believe that by breaking down the task of writing into stages—inventing or collecting data and ideas, planning, drafting, and revising, for example—writing tasks become more manageable. The *process* approach to teaching writing, adopted by many instructors in the 1970s and still the foundation of most composition programs, is based on a cognitive explanation of how people write. Students learn a set of strategies, such as *free writing*, which they can apply by themselves to manage each stage of the writing process. For example, students are taught "free writing"— a technique for generating ideas which urges students to write continuously and not edit their ideas or sentences.

During the last 30 years of research on the writing process some studies motivated us to revise early assumptions of the research of "writing process pioneers" like Janet Emig and Flowers and Hayes. We have learned that the writing process changes depending on the purpose for writing or the nature of the writing assignment and that the writing process often cannot be broken down into neat stages, but is recursive. For example, some researchers found that writers repeat the cycle of planning, drafting, and revising, over and over again (Perl). (See Chapter 5 for more information about cognitive theories and research.)

The cognitivists strongly influenced peer tutoring. All training programs for tutors focus heavily on the writing process. The planning, drafting, revision paradigm is often used as a heuristic for conducting writing conferences. For example, if there are few examples to support the ideas in an essay, the tutor may suggest that students return to the planning stage and identify examples they can use to improve the paper. In the 1970s and 1980s some writing center directors like Barrett Mandel, then the Director of the writing center at Rutgers University in New Jersey, based their tutoring programs on the writing process. When students first came to the writing center at Rutgers they practiced the various stages of the writing process over several sessions before focusing on a specific problem such as poor sentence construction which may have been the original reason they were sent to the writing center for help.

Social Constructionist Theory

While the writing process became the main focus of instruction in composition programs and writing centers, and also strongly influenced pedagogy (for example instructors respond to drafts and allow time for students to execute the various stages of the writing process), a group of composition specialists turned to social constructionist theory to explain how people learn to write. They asked the question, "To what degree are knowledge and learning social rather than individual?" (Kennedy 31). Their theories supported classroom pedagogies such as students reading each other's papers in class, and helped to explain and refine the interaction between the tutor and the tutee in writing centers. Many composition specialists believe that social constructionism offers the most comprehensive theory for teaching writing and explains better than cognitivist theories the reasons that peer tutoring works (Kennedy 368). In "Thinking and Writing as Social Acts" Bruffee summarizes the social constructionist position when he says,

> This essay assumes that there is no inherent, internal, universal mental structure that can work towards the "universals of sound reasoning." It assumes instead that what we call the universals of sound reasoning or a higher order reasoning ability is an internalization of language use or more broadly speaking the symbol use of certain human communities in particular our own literate Western European–American culture [. . .] (219)

When we write and how we write is governed by the language of the community of people within which we write, to whom we write. Writing—a form of conversation—begins in conversation and remains within that conversational community (214). In other words, to learn to write acceptable prose in college requires internalizing the *language* or languages of the academic community. By "languages" the social constructionist means not only the words and format of academic writing but the ideas about what constitutes evidence and acceptable frameworks for organizing that evidence. Furthermore, a major tenet of social constructionism is that writing is a form of *conversation*, which leads to the conclusion that it is through conversation that students best learn how to write. Patricia Bizzell, in "Academic Discourse: Taxonomy of Conventions or Collaborative Practice," says, "According to this model, it's as if the student attempting to master academic discourse was the new neighbor who steps up to a gossiping group at the church picnic, listens for awhile to get the hang of the conversation, and then tentatively joins in" (3).

By using examples of the kinds of questions teachers ask *themselves* as they try to frame the goals for writing instruction, Bruffee illustrates how teaching methods derived from social constructionist theory support peer tutoring. "For example, a cognitivist asks, 'What's going on in my students' heads?' And 'How can I get in there and change what's going on?' These are the questions implied when we wonder how to reach students, and how to implant in their heads what we believe is going on in our own" ("Conversation" 216). On the other hand, when a teacher believes that only if students feel themselves to be members of the academic community will they begin to think and write like academics, he or she will ask questions such as "How do I get my students to want to give up the values of the communities they are now members of, or at least every so often their loyalty to and dependence upon those communities? How do I help students to join another community in ways that make that change as comfortable and as fail safe as possible?" (216). One answer is to create a transitional community that diminishes the stress that comes with change while providing the opportunity for the student to experiment with the language (language with a big "L") and the thinking patterns or behaviors of the new community.

Peer tutors play an important role in establishing the transitional community that students may need to enter before becoming full-fledged members of the academic community. Bruffee believes that the most important expertise peer tutors gain in their training is the "linguistic flexibility required for helping students translate from one language to another—from the languages that peer tutors speak, the language of the transitional community, to the languages that faculty speak." He says, "Your [peer tutors] goal is to help tutees become fluent in the languages themselves, and in that way join the communities those languages constitute." In other words, students must learn both the process and conventions of academic writing which apply across disciplines, and in addition learn the special conventions of writing in their particular major ("Lost in Translation" 3).

The language of academic discourse is not easy to master. As Bruffee says, "students are already fluent in other languages that bear little resemblance to academic discourse; some of them speak fluent 'Dormitory,' for example. Some speak fluent 'Family and Home-Town,' although, of course, the family and home town languages they speak differ a good deal from family to family and from home town to home town." Faculty members are fluent in these too. But academic writing is distinct from conventional speech in many ways, most notably that academic writing demands greater explicitness of elaboration and a hierarchical rather than a merely sequential order of presentation. Proper use requires an awareness of audience as "other," and requires a context because the audience is unfamiliar with the circumstances of the writer's life and not privy to the writer's habit of thought. Peer tutors help students to understand this language, a language that Bruffee describes as a "linguistic picket fence," as well as how to use it. To quote him, "What peer tutors do in short, is to help tutees to find gates in linguistic picket fences and pass through them" ("Lost in Translation" 4).

In response to the question, "How can student peers, not themselves [full] members of the knowledge communities they hope to enter, help other students enter those communities," Bruffee responds,

> that while neither peer tutors nor their tutees may alone be masters of the normal discourse of a given knowledge community, by working together, by pooling their resources—they are very likely to be able to master it if their conversation is structured indirectly by the task or problem that a member of that community (the teacher) provides. (10)

The peer tutor has the advantage of being familiar with the general conventions of academic discourse. The student ideally "brings to the table" knowledge about the course and the writing assignment.

Currently most writing centers and other peer-tutoring programs explain the interaction between tutor and tutor using social constructionist theory. A conversation between the tutor and the tutee, where the tutee is encouraged to participate actively, is the method of peer tutoring endorsed by most writing centers and peer-tutoring programs. However, not everyone agrees. For example, Linda Shamoon and Deborah Burns call for more directiveness on the part of the peer tutor and suggest a less important role for the student. (For more information about some of the controversies related to peer tutoring, read my chapter on peer tutoring in *Writing Across the Curriculum and the New Millennium*.)

Why Peer Tutoring Works: The Research

Research on the effectiveness of peer tutoring grew from the broader category of research on collaborative learning. Sociologists Thomas M. Newcombe and Everett K. Wilson, in their study on the effects of peer influence on college students, say "Few students, we suspect, are immune to peer group influence, and we think such influence merits more study than it has received for both teacher and social scientist have a stake in the matter" (1966). The studies cited here reflect the variety of contexts in which collaborative learning and peer tutoring are successful:

- In 1960 M. L. J. Abercrombie published in the *Anatomy of Judgment* a study in which he found that peer group discussion was more effective than traditional instruction in teaching medical students the ability to make accurate diagnoses. Abercrombie said "there are very serious limitations on the extent to which a teacher can help a student to think as distinct from giving him a part of an established body of knowledge."

- In spite of the difficulty involved in measuring how much a student's writing improves as a direct result of a particular kind of instruction, studies during the last 30 years have demonstrated that the writing of students who work with peer groups improves as much as or more than the writing of students in traditional classrooms. A 1972 study by J. R. Lagana at the University of Pittsburgh showed that those students who received peer responses improved more rapidly in organization, critical thinking, and sentence revision, than students in classes in which their writing was read only by their instructors.

- In a 1990 study comparing the writing in tutored and nontutored classes, "Using a Peer Tutor to Improve Writing in Psychology Class," Judith Levine found that the papers written in the tutored class were better than the papers in the class that did not receive tutoring.

Several other studies on the effectiveness of peer tutoring on the college level demonstrate that peer tutoring is effective. For example, Smith found that peer tutoring improves the quality of the written product (1975), and Deming's study demonstrated that peer tutoring helps students develop more effective strategies for writing (1986).

Research on the Utility of Teacher–Student Conferences

In addition to studies on the effectiveness of tutoring, studies of the special benefits of conferences, although they often involved teachers rather than tutors, help us to understand the value of conferencing. For example, Kates (1977) and Sutton (1975) found that conferences lead to more positive attitudes toward writing instruction than writing classes. Some of the research on conferences was descriptive. Jacobs and Karliner (1977) described the discourse of conferences which leads to reflection and evaluation by the student. More recent studies try to explain why some conferences succeed and others fail. Newkirk (1995) found that conferences succeed when the tutor tolerates hesitancy or awkward responses. Another very interesting study suggests that conferences succeed when the methods employed there meet students' cultural expectations. For example, U.S. middle-class students prefer a less directive conversation, whereas African–American students and ESL students seem to favor a more directive approach (Pathey-Chavez and Ferris 1997). On the other hand, Walker and Elias (1987) discovered that a conference will fail if the instructor is too controlling.

What the Instructors Say

Observations of instructors who participate in programs like the Writing Fellows program at La Salle, where writing tutors are assigned to individual courses, are another source of information on their effectiveness. For example, note these comments by faculty at La Salle:

- "Kim Toomey did a really excellent job with my students. I am grateful to her." (Preston Feden, Education)
- "I spoke to you about keeping Karen for a whole year with my honors course. Please say this is O.K." (Joseph Volpe, Philosophy)
- "Rob has told me he will probably work with someone in the Department of Communication next semester. I understand his reasons completely and encourage him to do so, but I am very jealous of this instructor! Rob is so conscientious to interact with, helpful to me, and gives thoughtful suggestions to the students. They respect his comments. He did a superb job!" (Nancy Jones, Chemistry)

As I remarked in an essay which included a survey of peer-tutoring programs, "Comments like these are not unique to La Salle's peer-tutoring program. Directors of other peer-tutoring programs who responded to my survey reported almost unanimous faculty satisfaction with peer tutors' performance" (Soven WPA). Here are some representative comments of faculty connected to these peer-tutoring programs:

- Tremendous improvement in final products (John Bean, Seattle University).
- Improved performance of at-risk writers. GPAs in these classes [tutorial sections of freshman composition] equal those in regular classes, though students placed in them have lower essay and ACT scores (Janice Neulieb, Illinois State University).

Conclusion

Current practices of peer tutoring today are, or should be, guided by a rich body of theory and research only briefly described in this chapter. Unfortunately, some writing centers are still viewed as "fix it shops."

Stephen North, in "The Idea of a Writing Center" (1984), says that writing centers were never intended to be editing services or to have as their primary objective remediation, but a "place for active learning and student enrichment." He notes that despite the Herculean efforts of writing center directors, some faculty persist in this misguided notion.

This book takes its cue from the theories discussed in this chapter: the importance of individualizing education, the importance of students learning about themselves through writing, and the importance of learning how to write essays characterized by the conventions of academic discourses. Each student comes to the "peer-tutoring table" so to speak, with a unique set of language competencies and a variety of assumptions about college writing. Each student comes with ideas that they need help to express. No one is born knowing the strategies that are most useful for negotiating the writing process. No one is born knowing the conventions of academic writing. Not even the best students.

Every student can benefit from working with a writing tutor. As a writing tutor, you will help students examine their assumptions about writing and encourage them to learn the language of the academy. This text will train you to work with all kinds of writers, for example the basic writer, the good writer, the unmotivated writer, and writers whose first language is not English, but first [...] to the history of writing centers and Writing Fellows Programs and the basics of peer tutoring!

Questions for Discussion and Writing

1. Describe your assumptions about peer tutoring before reading this chapter.
2. How many "languages" do you speak, given Bruffee's definition? Can you describe some of the characteristics of at least one of these languages?
3. Write a description of your first year in college for a friend who is choosing a college.
4. Write a description of the freshman year experience at your school for a course on higher education. Interview students and incorporate their views in your paper.
5. Describe your experiences studying with your friends or helping them with their papers. If they have helped you with your papers describe your feelings as a "tutee."

Works Cited

Abercrombie, M. L. J. *Anatomy of Judgment*. Boston, MA: Brill Academic Publishers, 1980.

Bizzell, Patricia. "Academic Discourse: Taxonomy of Conventions or Collaborative Practice." Annual Meeting, *Conference on College Composition and Communication*. 1986. 1–9.

Brannon, Lil and Cy Knoblauch. *Rhetorical Tradition and Teaching Writing*. Upper Montclair, NJ: Boynton-Cook, 1984.

Bruffee, Kenneth. "Peer Tutoring and the 'Conversation of Mankind'." *Writing Centers: Theory and Administration*. Ed. Gary A. Olson. Urbana, IL: NCTE, 1984.

——. "Thinking and Writing as Social Acts." *Thinking, Reasoning, and Writing*. Ed. Elaine Maimon, Barbara Nodine, and Finbarr O'Connor. New York: Longman, 1989.

——. Kenneth. "Lost in Translation: Peer Tutors, Faculty Members, and the Art of Boundary Conversation," Tenth Anniversary Peer Tutoring Conference. Brown University, April 10 1993.

Clark, Irene Lurkis. "Maintaining Chaos in the Writing Center: A Critical Perspective on Writing Center Dogma." *Writing Center Journal* 11:1 (1990): 81–93.

Elbow, Peter. *Writing Without Teachers*. New York: Oxford University Press, 1973.

Emig, Janet. *The Composing Process of Twelfth Graders*. NCTE Report No. 13. Urbana, IL: NCTE, 1971.

Flower, Linda and John R. Hayes. "A Cognitive Process Theory of Writing." *College Composition and Communication* 32 (December, 1981): 365–387.

Harris, Muriel. *Teaching One to One. The Writing Conference*. Urbana, IL: National Council of Teachers of English, 1986.

Healy, Dave. "In the Temple of the Familiar: The Writing Center as Church." *Writing Center Perspectives*. Ed. Byron Stay, Christina Murphy, and Eric Hobson. Emmitsburg, MD: NCWA, 1995. 12–25.

Jacobs, S. and Karliner, A. "Helping Writers to Think: The Effects of Speech Roles in Individual Conferences on the Quality of Thought in Student Writing." *College English* 38(1977): 489–505.

Kates, J. "Individual Conferences Versus Typed Comments Without Conferences on Graded Composition Papers: The El Camino Experiment and the Compton Experiment." ERIC, No. ED 140 910, 1977.

Kennedy, Mary Lynch. Ed. *Theorizing Composition: A Critical Sourcebook of Theory and Scholarship in Contemporary Composition Studies.* Westport, CT: Greenwood Press, 1998.

Kinneavy, James, William McCleary, and James Nakadate. *Writing in the Liberal Arts Tradition.* New York: Harper and Row, 1985.

Lagana, G. "The Development, Implementation, and Evaluation of a Model for Teaching Composition Which Utilizes Individualized Learning and Peer Grouping." *DAI* 33 4063A ED 079 726.

Levine, J. R. "Using a Peer Tutor to Improve Writing in a Psychology Class: One Teacher's Experience." *Teaching of Psychology* 17:1 (1990): 57–58.

Macrorie, Ken. *Telling Writing.* Rochelle Park, NJ: Hayden Book Company, Inc., 1970.

Moffatt, Michael. *Coming of Age in New Jersey: College and American Culture.* New Brunswick, NJ: Rutgers University Press, 1989.

Newbcomb, Thomas M. and Everett K. Wilson. *College Peer Groups: Problems and Prospects for Research.* Chicago, IL: Aldine, 1966.

Newkirk, Thomas. "The Writing Conference as Performance." *Research in Teaching English* 29: 193–215.

North, Stephen. "The Idea of a Writing Center." *College English* 46 (1984): 433–446.

Pathey-Chavez, G. G. and D. R. Ferris. "Writing Conferences and the Weaving of Multivoiced Texts in Composition." *Research in Teaching English* 31: 51–90.

Perl, Sondra. Ed. *Landmark Essays on Writing Process.* Davis, CA: Hermagoras Press, 1994.

Pooley, Robert C. *Teaching English Grammar.* New York: Appleton-Century Crofts, 1946.

——. *Teaching English Usage.* New York: Appleton-Century Crofts, 1946.

Reigstad, Thomas and Donald A. McAndrew. *Training Tutors for Writing Conferences.* Urbana IL: NCTE, 1984.

Shamoon, Linda K. and Deborah H. Burns. "A Critique of Peer Tutoring." *Writing Center Journal* 15:2 (1995): 134–151.

Smith, M. E. *Peer Tutoring in a Writing Workshop.* Doctoral Dissertation, University of Michigan. *DAI* 35 3623A.

Sommers, Nancy. "Revision of Student Writers and Experienced Adult Writers." *The Writing Teacher's Sourcebook.* 2nd ed. Eds. Gary Tate and Edward Corbett. New York: Oxford University Press, 1988.

Soven, Margot. "Curriculum Based Peer Tutoring: A Survey."
    WPA:Writing Program Adminstration 17:1–2 (1993): 58–74.
——. *Teaching Writing in Middle and Secondary Schools.* Needham
    Heights, MA: 1999.
——. "Curriculum Based Tutors and WAC." *WAC for the New
    Millennium.* Ed. McLeod, Miraglia, Soven, Thaiss. Urbana,
    IL: NCTE, 2001.
Sutton, D. G. "Evaluating Teaching Methods in Composition." Paper
    Presented at the Annual Meeting of the Conference on College
    Composition and Communication. March, St. Louis, MO: Eric
    Document Reproduction Service, No. ED 120–730, 1975.
Walker, C. P. and D. Elias. "Writing Conference Talk: Factors Associated
    with High and Low Rated Writing Conferences." *Research in
    Teaching English* 21: 266–285.
Warnock, John and Tilly Warnock. "Liberatory Writing Centers:
    Rostering Authority to Writers." *Writing Centers: Theory and
    Administration.* Ed. Gary Olson. Urbana, IL: NCTE, 1984. 16–23.

For Further Reading

Bruffee, Kenneth. *A Short Course in Writing: Composition, Collaborative
    Learning, and Collaborative Reading.* 4th ed. New York: Harper
    Collins, 1993.
Goodlad, Sinclair and Beverly Hirst. *Peer Tutoring: A Guide to Learning
    by Teaching.* New York: Nichols Publishing, 1989.
Kinkead, Joyce and Jeanette Harris. Ed. *Writing Centers in Context.*
    Urbana, IL: NCTE, 1993.
Mullin, Joan and Ray Wallace, Ed. *Intersections: Theory and Practice in
    the Writing Center.* Urbana, IL: NCTE, 1994.
Soliday, Mary. "Shifting Roles in Classroom Tutoring: Cultivating the
    Art of Boundary Crossing." *Writing Center Journal.* 16:1 (1995):
    58–73.

2

Where We Tutor—
How We Tutor

In this chapter I discuss the history of writing centers and Writing Fellows (course-linked tutors) Programs and their distinctive features and give a brief introduction to online tutoring, which is discussed in detail in Chapter 8. Then I review important aspects of the peer-tutoring process that apply regardless of how and where the tutoring takes place, the ethics of peer tutoring and some of the principles which form the basis of all peer-tutoring practice, the importance of getting acquainted, the significance of responding to students' papers as readers, not as mini-instructors but as sympathetic peers, and finally I end this chapter with a student's view of his role as a peer tutor.

Once you have practiced the methods introduced in this chapter, you will have what I call peer-tutoring survival skills. Even if you are not sure how to identify all the problems in a paper, you will know "tutor speak." You will be able to recognize many of the problems in students' papers even before you read Chapter 3, where I talk about conferencing and written comments, and Chapter 5, where I focus on specific problems such as weaknesses in organization, development and coherence issues that affect the whole paper, and sentence level issues such as style, syntax, and common errors.

Learning how to tutor is like learning to write. The process is recursive. You can't learn everything at once. It's the dialogue between this text, your experience as a tutor, and your instructor's guidance that will lead you to the promised land of expert tutors.

Here we go!

Welcome to the Writing Center: Past and Present

Until the early 1990s almost all peer tutors in writing worked in writing centers. As of 1996 there were writing centers on more that 90 percent of the campuses in the United States (Grimm 523). Today, although it is still probably true that most students who receive help from a peer tutor see him or her in a writing center, peer tutoring online is becoming increasingly popular as more writing centers offer online services ("OWL" stands for Online Writing Center). But the number of Writing Fellows programs continues to grow (Soven-Survey). In these programs tutors are assigned to individual courses and read the drafts of all students in a particular course.

But let's back up a bit to the history of writing centers and Writing Fellows Programs. In "Early Writing Centers: Toward a History," Peter Carino notes that tracing writing center history "since the inception of the *Writing Lab Newsletter* in 1977 and the *Writing Center Journal* three years later [...] is not difficult" (103). However, writing centers did exist before the 1970s, when they were usually called writing clinics or writing labs. As Carino says, although early descriptions of these centers suggest that they were grammar fix-it-shops, his research indicates that the history of the writing center is far more complicated than that (104).

He claims that the origin of writing centers is to be found in the classroom: As early as 1904, a classroom method known as the *laboratory method* was used to teach writing. In classes characterized by the laboratory method, students were given individual help from the instructor and peer editing groups were a part of writing instruction, "techniques at the heart of writing center methodology today" (105). He credits a high school teacher, Philo Buck, as possibly having coined the term *laboratory method*. By 1917 an article by Frank W. Cady of Middlebury College confirms that the laboratory method had also been implemented on the college level. The writing lab during this period was viewed as a place where all students could benefit. Cady emphasized the value of individual writing instruction. He says, "As all of the work is individual we build on individual error, calling a student's attention only to errors which he himself makes" (111). Furthermore, he makes it clear that the instruction in the lab would not be confined to the sentence level, but focus on rhetorical problems that "call for detailed thinking and discussion" (110).

Carino's study leads him to believe that until the 1930s the writing lab remained confined to the classroom. However, in 1934 the University of Minnesota and the State University of Iowa (now the University of Iowa) situated writing lab pedagogy in a facility separate from the classroom, probably for the historical reason that during the 1930s the college population expanded to include the children of immigrants, many of whom were identified as ill prepared for college. At the same time John Dewey's philosophy of education which stressed individualizing education reinforced the writing lab movement (106). Also, the number of free-standing writing labs increased as a result of Armed Forces English—on-campus programs for preparing officers for World War II (107). These programs were designed to give officers two years of training in English in two semesters. The army insisted that students learn at their own pace, a method that many schools then continued after the war because of its success.

By the 1950s writing centers were becoming more of an integral part of college writing programs. The GI Bill made it possible for many students to attend college. These returning students needed help with their writing. Although many of these early writing centers focused on remediation, the philosophy of writing centers was changing. Dorothy Whitted at Ohio Wesleyan presented a view of students that reflects contemporary writing center philosophy: "The student is not someone who fails to meet a mythical arbitrary standard of excellence, but is a non-member of an in-group with respect to communication in an academic context" (109). Whitted sounds very much like a social constructionist. Open enrollment, which permitted all students with a high school diploma to go to any college in the CUNY (City University of New York) system in the 1960s, increased exponentially the number of writing centers committed to this philosophy.

Early writing centers did not use undergraduate writing tutors, though some used graduate students who worked with a faculty member. It would take the vision of people like Bruffee and Harris to join the two ideas that form the philosophical foundation for contemporary writing centers: the power of collaborative work with a peer (the transitional community Bruffee recommended) in a setting which provides individualized instruction.

Welcome to the Writing Fellows Program: Peer Tutoring in the Future?

Writing Fellows programs and writing centers both trace their history back to the one-on-one approach developed in classrooms as early as 1904. The teachers using this approach were advised to behave like peers. One instructor using the lab approach reports with obvious satisfaction that one of his students said, "You aren't the dignified teacher I used to think you were. You seemed like one of the boys, and I have learned to like English in laboratory work" (Carino 104). The classroom laboratory approach had much in common with current Writing Fellows programs, since all students had the opportunity for lab instruction, regardless of their competency. (All students in Writing Fellows–assisted courses are required to participate in the program.)

In "The Politics of Peer Tutoring," Kail and Trimbur point out that the first Writing Fellows programs which employed peer tutors and where instruction did not take place in the classroom were attached to first-year composition programs. Students were required to work one-on-one with a peer tutor in addition to attending class. Mary Soliday reported in 1995 that this was the case at the City College of New York. Some freshman composition programs still include this requirement. For example, at La Salle University, students in special sections of freshman composition for underprepared students work with peer tutors as part of the course.

However, in the mid-1980s, which saw the rapid development of Writing Across the Curriculum (WAC) programs, Writing Fellows Programs began assigning tutors to courses in all disciplines. When I was first introduced to the concept of course-linked tutoring in writing, it seemed to me that curriculum-based peer tutoring (the more generic name for Writing Fellows programs) was the obvious next step in WAC programs like the one at La Salle University and many other institutions. Because the major goal of WAC programs was to involve all instructors in all disciplines in the improvement of writing skills, faculty development was the cornerstone of WAC programs (for example Western Washington University, Lafayette College, and George Mason University). In the WAC faculty workshops instructors were encouraged to use a process approach to writing in their courses and to urge their students to think of revision as an integral part of the writing process. What could be more natural then assigning a Writing Fellow to instructors to help them read drafts?

For several reasons the growth of Writing Fellows programs has not been as rapid as the development of writing centers. Most Writing Fellows programs require that students enroll in a course, whereas the training for a writing center position is often more limited. In addition faculty sponsors need to be recruited. They play a larger roll in the program than they do in schools where writing tutoring is limited to Writing Centers. But most important of all, to start a Writing Fellows program, you need a composition specialist interested in developing and administering the program and teaching the course for training Writing Fellows.

Tutoring in the Writing Center

If you are tutoring in a writing center you will meet students in a one-on-one conference, also called a face-to-face conference, sometimes abbreviated to "f2f." Many of them will come voluntarily to the writing center during the stage of writing paper when they need the most help. The student who "has no idea where to begin" may drop in unannounced, or the student who wants someone to edit the paper for mechanics may appear an hour before the paper is due. Most writing centers have policies that protect their peer tutors from becoming human spell-checkers. Some students may visit the center several times, and some may come only once. Don't be offended. Remember what I said in the Introduction: students have complicated lives. A writing assignment may not be a student's first priority when she has just broken up with her boy friend. I'm sure this comes as no surprise to you!

Some students will come to the writing center because they are required to go or advised to get help by their instructors. A colleague of mine at La Salle is well known for "walking" her students to the writing center right after class. These students may come unwillingly or, then again, they may be relieved that someone has noticed that they have a writing problem. Students who have problems writing are usually aware of them, but often don't know how to get help, or are too embarrassed to ask for assistance.

There are many advantages to writing center tutoring. If the student walks in voluntarily, he is bound to be motivated. Also, he may be able to get immediate help just when he needs it. Of course, another advantage is that you are meeting face to face, which makes it easy to get acquainted. (I have more to say about the *getting acquainted* stage of the tutoring process in Chapter 3.) On the other hand there are disadvantages. For example, you may not know much about the assignment that is the prompt for the paper. Even if the student has it with him, the assignment may be confusing. You'll need to *psyche out* the instructor's expectations. Sometimes the student will have left it in his dorm room. Or perhaps the teacher did not write out the instructions for the assignment, but explained it in class—possibly the worst case scenario unless the student has a very good memory.

Writing Fellows Programs

Those of you training to be Writing Fellows, or Writing Associates as they are called at the University of Pennsylvania and Swarthmore College, will be in a very different situation than writing center tutors. You will be assigned to read the drafts of all the students in a specific course, not just those students who demonstrate weak writing skills. In many Writing Fellows programs, the tutors first read the drafts, write comments on the papers, and then meet with the student to review the comments and discuss the paper (for example La Salle University, Brown University, Brigham Young University, and others).

As you can imagine, in Writing Fellows Programs, the conference serves a different function than the drop-in conference in a writing center. One of the major questions for Writing Fellows is how to conduct the conference when they have already written comments on the draft.

But this system has a built-in time lag, which may or may not be beneficial. The Brown University Guidelines, adapted by many other Writing Fellows programs, recommends giving the tutor about a week to read the drafts and hold conferences with the students. Many instructors at La Salle believe that, because this system requires the student to begin thinking about the paper ahead of time rather than the night before it's due, they get better papers. On the other hand, the time lag (while the Writing Fellow is reading the papers) may be a disadvantage because the writer may have forgotten what he wrote or why he wrote it!

There are other significant advantages to Writing Fellows program. The Writing Fellow is typically responding to a draft, even if it is a hastily written one. The student has at least done some of the work before meeting with the tutor. At La Salle we require that students submit a draft as a condition of working with the Writing Fellow. If the student is having trouble getting started, we suggest a trip to the writing center *before* meeting with the Writing Fellow. The writing center is a better place for help when getting started.

Due to the way they are structured, Writing Fellows programs may allow the tutor to be more informed (about the paper) than he can be if tutoring in a writing center: The tutor and student usually meet at least twice during the semester. At La Salle we require instructors who request the assistance of a Writing Fellow to assign at least two papers. The Writing Fellows at La Salle often say that the second round often goes better than the first because they know the students. But if you tutor at a writing center, you may see the student only once.

Also, the Writing Fellow is usually very familiar with the writing assignment. The instructor of the course to which the Writing Fellow has been assigned typically gives the Writing Fellow a copy of the assignment and discusses his evaluation criteria. (We'll have more to say about faculty expectations in Chapter 6.)

Tutoring at its Best: What the Experts Say

Composition specialists who favor the writing center model focus on who initiates the action, the teacher or the student. Kail and Trimbur concede that in the "curriculum-based model [Writing Fellows Programs] more students see tutors [...] and the program is easier to administer" (7). However, they believe that "the curriculum-based model inhibits collaboration because tutors are seen as part of the institution and share its authority" (7). In other words, the advantages typically associated with peer tutoring are compromised when peer tutoring is connected to courses because the student is required to participate.

On the other hand, those who favor the Writing Fellows model focus on these advantages: Writing Fellows programs eliminate the stigma often felt by students who seek help at the writing center. Curriculum- or class-based tutoring reinforces the idea that revision is an integral part of the writing process. Although most writing centers welcome all students, in fact most students come or are advised to go to a writing center only because they have a problem. Their image of themselves as poor writers may be reinforced by a trip to the writing center. Haring-Smith points out that because "All students in a given course work with peer tutors regardless of abilities, no student need identify herself or be identified by a faculty member as needing help in order to participate in this program" (178). Not only can all students benefit from a "second pair of eyes" but, in addition, Writing Fellows programs underscore the importance of revision, regardless of writing ability.

Writing Fellows also have a more direct impact on instructors' assignments than do tutors in writing centers who may never meet instructors. When we ask faculty who have worked with a Writing Fellow for a semester whether the Fellow influenced their future assignments, invariably the answer is "yes." Writing Fellows often detect pitfalls in an assignment sometimes missed by the instructor.

As with any teaching innovation, there are benefits and limitations to Writing Fellows Programs. Until we have additional studies comparing voluntary tutoring to required tutoring, we must assume that both kinds of tutoring help students learn to write but perhaps in different ways. It's reasonable to assume that the relationship between tutor and student is affected by the differences between voluntary tutoring and required tutoring. However, both forms of tutoring send an important message about your school's commitment to good writing. Whether you see students in a writing center or as a Writing Fellow assigned to a course, whether you work with them online or in one-on-one conferences, you help your school convey that message.

Online Tutoring ("Send Your Paper as an Attachment")

If you are tutoring online, students will contact you when they are having trouble getting started or, for that matter, any time thereafter while they are working on their paper. Of course, in contrast to tutoring in a writing center, in addition to never having met the student, you will be responding in writing to a student who is not sitting in front of you. On the other hand, online tutoring may encourage honesty. Some students are too shy to meet in person.

Online tutoring or online teaching of writing takes different forms at different schools. In some cases entire writing courses are taught online. The University of Pennsylvania recently completed a comparative study of an online freshman composition course with the traditionally taught freshman writing seminars. Penn is considering offering online writing courses as an alternative to the standard class based freshman writing seminar.

The most common form of online tutoring uses email, called asynchronous communication in "electronic-speak." Students send their drafts as attachments and wait for a response from the tutor. However, some schools (for example Purdue University) are experimenting with electronic communication programs that allow for synchronous communication (give and take real-time chat between student and tutor) in one window while allowing the tutor and student to view the text in another window. Additional studies are needed to compare the advantages of different approaches to online tutoring. I'll talk more about online tutoring in Chapter 8.

Friend, Tutor, or Mini-Instructor?

There is widespread agreement on the ethics of peer tutoring, no matter what the tutoring context. Leigh Ryan (*The Bedford Guide for Writing Tutors*) is right on target when he says, "Tutoring students can be an exciting, enjoyable, and rewarding experience. It is also a professional activity involving both responsibility and trust." Accordingly, tutors should observe certain principles of conduct in their relationships with students, teachers, and other tutors. Of the principles that Ryan recommends, these are the ones that I think are most important: Never comment negatively about teacher's teaching methods, assignments, personality or grading policies; never suggest a grade for a paper; never criticize the grade the teacher has given a paper; and honor the confidentiality of the peer-tutoring relationship (1–3).

Although you may feel that adhering to these guidelines may at times make you feel less like a peer, keep in mind that you are playing several roles. At times they may seem at odds with one another. As a peer you talk with your friends about your teachers. But once you put on your tutoring hat, you must also consider your relationship with the faculty, which if poor can undermine the peer-tutoring program. It's true that being a peer tutor may sometimes seem like a balancing act, but very few roles in life are simple. My primary role is "teacher," but at times I am "friend" and at times I'm asked to be a confidante to my students. However, I need to know where to draw the line. You face a similar challenge.

The Language of Peer Tutoring: Let's Get Acquainted

Whether you are introducing yourself to a class, or saying "hello" to a student who has come to the writing center for the first time or has sent his first message to you online, be sure to tell students about yourself. They will be curious to know who you are and why you decided to become a peer tutor. If you are tutoring one-on-one, you may want to break the ice by exchanging information about majors, extracurricular activities, and so on. Be sure to demonstrate your enthusiasm for peer tutoring. Indicate that you look forward to working with the student or with the whole class if you are a Writing Fellow. Ask students if they have any questions about how peer tutoring works. If not, then explain what it is that writing tutors do. You might say something like,

> My role is to give you some suggestions, to the best of my knowledge. I am not
> an expert, but I've been chosen to be a writing tutor, because my instructors
> believe that I am a good writer. You may accept or reject my advice. Your

paper is still your responsibility. If you have any questions about my comments, for example, or are not sure that I helped you understand the assignment, talk with your instructor. Please don't ask me to predict your grade. That puts me in an awkward position. Also, one of the rules about peer tutoring is that we are not supposed to discuss your attitudes about your teacher or their assignments.

It's important that students understand the ethics of peer tutoring as well as the potential benefits of working with a writing tutor.

OK, We're Acquainted: Now What Do I Say?

Remember this simple principle, and you are on your way to becoming a great tutor: *Evaluation* and *Response* are two different activities. Evaluation is your assessment of the paper. Response is what you say to the student. Once you have evaluated the paper, you must decide how to communicate your assessment to the writer. Rarely will you give the student a blow-by-blow account of your evaluation.

Even a barrage of readerly comments such as "I'm confused" or "Could you explain this point with another example?" can be overwhelming. My favorite example of the barrage syndrome, though at the time I would not have used the word "favorite," occurred many years ago when I was writing the proposal for my doctoral dissertation. My advisor returned the draft covered with green (not red!) ink. The color didn't matter. His intent was virtuous—to help me write a good dissertation. The results were catastrophic. I never looked at that proposal again, and in fact it took me several years before I had the courage to write a new one. In all fairness, there were other factors besides all that green ink which were responsible for the delay. But the green ink didn't help.

The remainder of this chapter will focus on response: the kinds of comments made by the tutor that are the most beneficial for motivating students to revise and the danger of too much criticism, whether it's in writing or during a conference. We will also discuss methods for responding to carelessly written drafts, partial drafts, or no drafts at all! (Online commenting will be covered in Chapter 8.)

The Transparent Reader Approach

It's helpful to think about three levels of response when tutoring writing. The first level is the *transparent reader* approach. This means responding more like an ordinary reader who is attempting to understand the paper, rather than as a writing instructor who is reading the paper to evaluate it. For example, you might say, "I'm confused, could you please explain this statement. I need an example" rather than the puzzling "poor development" comment often used by instructors, As Walvoord says, "In using this approach, always remember that writing is not 'wrong' in the same way that 'two plus two equals five is wrong.' Instead, writing can more accurately be said to fail when it does not effectively communicate to its intended reader" (146).

A three-level response approach, suggested by Walvoord, in which you first identify the appropriate level of response based on both the student's ability and your understanding of the paper, has several advantages. If you think the student can revise without much help you can limit your response to readerly comments such as those in p. 30. This is a first-level response. You are assuming that "the student is capable of finding solutions to the writing problems that provoke your negative reactions and repeating the successes that spur you to praise" (147). Responding on this level assumes that the student can recognize the problem causing the reader's confusion and knows how to solve it.

Sometimes, you will give a first-level response when you sense a problem without being able to identify it, or if you can identify it, you may not know how to solve it. Be honest when this happens. It's one of those times when you can convince the student that you are indeed a peer, not a writing instructor.

The second-level response is appropriate when either the condition of the paper or what you know about the student tells you that the student needs additional help beyond the readerly response "I'm confused." On the second level, you not only express your reaction as a reader but also explain the reasons for your reactions. In other words you identify the problem causing your confusion rather than leave it up to the writer to identify the problem. Walvoord gives these examples: "I got lost here because you did not indicate clearly enough the relationships between these two statements" or "This paragraph avoids monotony because you varied the length and construction of your sentences" or "I had to read this sentence twice because there are two possible ways to interpret it" (247).

On the third-level response, you begin by responding as a reader, not only identifying the problem but also suggesting how to solve it. Again, Walvoord's example is useful: "I got lost here. Try inserting a word or phrase to clarify the relationship between these two ideas" (247). Even at the third level you are giving the writer recommendations, not answers. You are not supplying the word in this case but indicating the need for a word.

In general, your comments should encourage self-sufficiency. Always begin by raising questions, rather than offering advice. For example, the following question asks the student to reconsider the organization of the paper: "Did you consider placing the description of the house elsewhere in the paper?"

The transparent reader approach to comments, which suggests that you always begin with your reaction as a reader (for example "I'm not sure what you mean" or "I don't understand the connection between this idea and the next one"), whether they are written or oral, conveys the idea that writing is always written for a reader. It sends the message to the student that there is no such thing as "poor coherence" or "poor development" in isolation from a specific text written for a specific purpose to a specific reader. For example, one might need only one example to illustrate an idea, which is familiar to the reader, but several examples may be necessary if the idea is new or very complex to the intended readers.

Be Positive, But Be Honest!

In "In Praise of Praise," the landmark essay by Paul Diederich, which was one of the first essays to focus on the importance of praise, the author says we know that teachers are very good at telling students what is wrong with their papers, but they are very stingy when it comes to praise. It's as important for students to know when their writing is successful as it is for them to know when to revise. Many students assume that they are poor writers. I know that many students enter my office saying, "I know my paper isn't good. My worst subject is English." You want to be careful not to reinforce such feelings. Also, as Walvoord points out, the teacher (or in this case the tutor) who does not give praise "throws away an excellent instructional method—telling students when they have done right." I agree with her observation that "A student often hits on good writing only half consciously, like a blindfolded birthday child who heads toward the right part of the donkey but honestly doesn't know the tail's going in the proper place unless the audience squeals. The teacher [tutor] ought to describe the successes, so that the student can repeat them consciously next time" (149).

Sometimes, in their zeal to not overlook any mistakes, tutors can be as discouraging as some instructors. One of our writing tutors at La Salle was appalled by the writing of his peers, and, without meaning to do so, he conveyed that message to them. We got comments back on the Student Surveys at the end of the semester such as "Joe [not his real name] thinks I am dumb. He makes too many corrections on my papers." Fortunately Joe was an isolated case.

Most tutors are more like Eric DePaul, another tutor at La Salle, who writes in his report on his tutoring experiences.

> When marking the drafts, I was often tempted to simply state what the student had done wrong and then move on to the next sentence or paragraph. However, aiming at writing commentary that would not offend and be helpful as possible, I suppressed my desires and consistently began my comments with either "I think that [. . .]" or "You seem to have [. . .]"

On the other hand, tutors must be honest. You shouldn't praise the paper or part of the paper unless it deserves praise. You will find yourself wanting to say something nice about a student's paper. Don't go overboard. The axiom that you can always find something positive to say about all papers is not true. Some drafts have no redeeming features. It's dangerous not to be honest. You will rapidly lose your credibility with students if the instructor gives the essay a "D" when you led the student to believe that his essay needed very little revising. To avoid this pitfall avoid general comments, such as "Your draft is on its way; you are almost there!" and superlatives such as "This is a great introduction!" You are less apt to mislead students and get yourself in hot water with instructors if you limit your compliments to specific parts of the paper and use qualifiers liberally ("I *think* this is a good introduction. It gets my interest.").

Conclusion

Once you start tutoring, you can begin to integrate the advice in this chapter with your own tutoring experiences. Steve Martin did just that after his first round meeting with 15 students. His description of the process is so interesting that I have attached it as an appendix to this chapter. Although Steve tried to use many of the recommendations in this chapter, he does what all good tutors should do; he uses his own categories for summarizing those which he finds most helpful.

Questions for Writing or Discussion

1. As with writing, there's no need to learn everything about peer tutoring before you meet your first student or read your first student paper. If you do not need to begin tutoring immediately, start by reading a friend's paper and practice "getting acquainted" and giving a readerly response to an essay he is working on. See how it feels to use "tutor speak."

2. How do you feel about using the services of your school's writing center?
3. If you have utilized the services of a writing center describe your experience.
4. If your school has a Writing Fellows program, and you have been in a class which had the assistance of a Writing Fellow, describe your experience.
5. Interview several students who voluntarily came to the writing center for help. Ask them to describe their experiences.
6. Ask permission to observe a peer-tutoring session at your school's Writing Center. Using Steve Martin's categories, describe the approach of a peer tutor in the writing center. (His paper appears at the end of the chapter.)

Works Cited

Carino, Peter. "Early Writing Centers: Toward a History." *Writing Center Journal* 15:2 (1995): 103–115.

Diederich, Paul. "In Praise of Praise." *A Guide for Evaluating Composition*. Urbana, IL: NCTE, 1965.

Grimm, Nancy. "Rearticulating the Work of the Writing Center." *College Composition and Communication* 47:4 (1996): 523–485.

Haring-Smith, Tori. "Changing Students' Attitudes: Writing Fellows Program." *Writing Across the Curriculum: A Guide for Developing Programs*. Ed. S.H. McLeod and Margot Soven, Newbury Park, CA: Sage, 1992. 175–188.

Kail, Harvey and John Trimbur. "The Politics of Peer Tutoring." *WPA: Writing Program Administration* 11:1–2 (1987): 5–12.

Martin, Stephen. "Write and Wrong: The First Round," Paper Written for English 360: Writing and the University, La Salle University, 2002.

Ryan, Leigh. *The Bedford Guide for Writing Tutors*. 2nd ed. Boston, MA: Bedford Books, 1998.

Soliday, Mary. "Shifting Roles in Classroom Tutoring: Cultivating the Art of Boundary Crossing." *Writing Center Journal* 16:1 (1995): 59–73.

Soven, Margot. "Curriculum Based Peer Tutoring Programs: A Survey." *WPA: Writing Program Administration*. 17:1–2 (1993): 58–74.

Walvoord, Barbara Fassler. *Helping Students Write Well.* 2nd ed.
New York: MLA, 1986.

For Further Reading

Barnett, Robert W. and Jacob S. Blumner. *The Allyn and Bacon Guide to
Writing Center Theory and Practice.* Needham Heights, MA:
Longman, 2000.

Boquet, Elizabeth H. *Noise from the Writing Center.* Logan, UT: Utah
State University Press, 2002.

Faigley, Lester. "Writing Centers in Times of Whitewater." *Writing
Center Journal* 19:1 (1998): 7–18.

Pemberton, Michael A. and Joyce Kinkead, Ed. *The Center Will Hold.*
Logan, UT: Utah State University Press, 2003.

Raines, Helen Howell. "Tutoring and Teaching: Continuum,
Dichotomy, or Dialectic." *Writing Center Journal* 14:2 (1994):
150–162.

Appendix: "Write and Wrong: The First Round" by Steve Martin

Perhaps the greatest folly of philosophers is their tendency to persecute upstarts and beginners, shredding to pieces bright ideas that happen to be clouded by flawed logic or sketchy premises or vague conclusions. While good philosophy takes such things into account, good philosophers find the bright spots first. So this was my challenge, to see my first round of papers not as puzzles formed by many little mistake-shaped pieces, but as gnarled oysters with philosophical pearls inside.

The success of writing fellowship hinges on the fellow's understanding of her roles as supporter, guide, and motivator. This paper will demonstrate how I gradually came to grips with these three facets of fellowship, and delineate the circumstances and consequences that resulted from my attempts to fulfill these roles. As supporter, the tutor must seek and find the praiseworthy elements of the tutee's paper. As guide, the tutor must correctly identify those aspects of a student's paper that are deficient. As motivator, the tutor must present this information in a way that encourages the students to revise their writing. Using these roles as a standard, I can assess my effectiveness as a Writing Fellow.

Before delving into the details of my performance, I should note some important information about the background of my tutorship. I am assigned to Dr. Marc Moreau's Philosophy 151D-AO1: The Human Person class. The class is a basic introduction-to-philosophy course geared toward students with little to no background in philosophy. Dr. Moreau laid out a pretty clear task for his class: "Your assignment is to develop the contrast between wisdom and intelligence with the aim of determining which of these two qualities is the more valuable possession. The assignment is to be treated as an effort at persuasion. Your goal is to persuade reasonable readers that the position you develop is a sensible one [. . .]" As one could imagine, this is a simple assignment that is not in the least bit easy. Wisdom and intelligence do not fit snugly into any definition, but they do, however, make for great philosophizing.

Fellowship of Support

Supporter is the first and foremost role of the Writing Fellow because it challenges the tutor to look at the tutee's paper in terms of potential, requires the tutor to concentrate on positive aspects of the paper, and provokes the tutor into framing the paper around these positives.

Richard Larson, Ben McClelland, Frank O'Hare, Peter Elbow, and Anne Gere, among others, all make sure to praise a paper before launching into any type of criticism. I adopted the maxim, "If you can't write something positive about the paper in the first line of comments, then you haven't read the paper well enough." This little rule ensured that I read each paper with an open mind, rather than bury it with a sharp criticism right off the bat. Dr. Joe Volpe has said that all philosophy should be read like a student's paper—carefully, joyfully, and with critical appreciation.

A Volpese corollary is that if a reader enters a philosophical work with the intent to destroy, he will find a way to destroy it. In the same sense, if a Writing Fellow enters into a student paper with the intent to scratch out and cross off, he will find a way to scratch out and cross off the paper itself. Some papers are more difficult to extol right away; in fact, I read quite a few of them. Ironically, the paper that I initially found to be the weakest turned out, upon close inspection, to contain highly profound philosophical perspectives. At first reading, the paper appeared shallow at best. Through a series of short paragraphs, the student defined wisdom and intelligence using the ever-popular paper starter, *Webster's New Collegiate Dictionary*. This rather cliché intro, which lacked a thesis statement, jumped from the theoretical discussion of the nature of wisdom and intelligence to a rant about the failings of an American society that does not respect the elderly, and a seemingly self-gratifying recognition of his own intelligence and lack of wisdom. Then the paper ended.

But I gave the paper a second look. Then I started to see its potential. There was no thesis statement because he was developing it as he wrote. The Webster's definitions were catalysts: "I can't put these ideas into words, so I'll turn to a standard definition and build my paper off critiques of those standards." His short paragraphs early on actually denoted a neat philosophical style: a step-by-step, reader-friendly progression into his paper. When I tried to understand the significance of his weighing wisdom and intelligence via real world examples, I was stunned at where I arrived. His philosophical position *could* be a recognition that philosophical concepts can only be measured by their place in the material world. He is a philosopher of action, one who sees philosophy as potential, and behavior as actualization of philosophy. From this position, wisdom and intelligence can *only* be evaluated empirically, through experience. He does exactly that, first comparing western-favored youth to eastern-favored filial piety. He then moves from the macro to the micro, sighting examples in his own life that demonstrate an experiential valuing of wisdom and intelligence.

As supporter, I could see through mistakes into the heart of some very deep concepts. I could highlight these concepts and hopefully make them clear for the students as well. By opening all of my written comments with praise, I feel that I made my subsequent criticisms easier to grasp. Although the portion of my comments dealing with praise was normally limited to a short paragraph, reading the papers in this context directed my criticisms.

Fellowship of Guidance

As a guide, the tutor must be able not only to identify problems with the paper but also to carefully show the writer what those problems are and demonstrate how they can be addressed. Most of my written comments serve my role as guide in the writing process. My strategy was to pinpoint three clear and distinct deficiencies, and then explain them as simply as I could. Rarely stepping beyond Barbara Walvoord's second level of response, I most often applied critical thinking questions to the student's paper, with my suggestions for change as an afterthought. My thinking was that it would be too much to start suggesting changes without having satisfactorily discussed, in the conference, what was wrong.

When I wrapped up my last conference, I felt a slight pang of anxiety. "Have I taken all of the personality out of these papers and inserted my own notions of a good paper in their place? Have I essentially co-written the same paper nine times?" I became worried because every student had essentially the same problems: no real thesis, thus, little to no thesis statement; conclusions that don't follow from premises; shifting definitions; broad generalizations. I theorized that these were all effects of one cause: first-time philosophers learning how to write philosophy. After a bit of reflection, combined with a look at a student's second draft, I understood that each of my students would certainly retain their own conception of what the paper should be, perhaps with some basic tools that I had hopefully provided for everyone with which I worked. If this meant that every paper landed on Dr. Moreau's desk with a thesis statement, introduction and conclusion, solid examples, and clear points of discussion, so be it. Maybe it's a bit arrogant to think those are uniquely elements of my paper to begin with.

I suppose the biggest strength of the papers that I read was their tendency to experiment with concepts, with language, with approaches to the assignment. While each paper could be roughly framed by an Introduction–Body (Wisdom/Intelligence/Contrast)–Conclusion format, and every paper's thesis was essentially the same ("Wisdom is knowledge gained from experience, intelligence is knowledge gained from books, formulae, and so on, and wisdom is more valuable, but less valued"), each paper varied greatly in its modus operandi. It would seem that freshmen are much less afraid to say things in strange and fantastic and often absurdly broad ways than more experienced students. Although this easily leads to gratuitous errors, it also allows for a certain freedom of thought and interpretation.

As far as weaknesses go, they ranged greatly. All the papers that I read demonstrated poor language mechanics (mainly grammar and usage), unclear development of a thesis, shifting definitions, and scattershot structure. Some papers exhibited conclusions that differed from premises, outlandishly sweeping declarations about human nature, and organization that needed organizing. A preliminary discussion with Dr. Moreau, along with my own instinct, behooved me to prioritize points of interest for my comments. My feeling was usually that if the student could create a strong thesis statement, using developed points from the body of the paper, much would fall into place. I tried to point out that the thesis statement can be used as a measuring stick for every statement in the paper: "If what you're about to write does not agree with the thesis statement, then we must figure out why they don't go together, adjust what you're going to write, or rethink the thesis of the paper." The one student who came to me with her postconference revision did just that: construct a strong thesis statement and pick through what she had written with that statement in mind. Besides improving her paper, her extra work really made me feel as if I had helped her.

Thesising, as I like to say, seems to lead into other areas of structure and organization that I felt a need to pinpoint in most papers. As far as mechanics go, I placed at the bottom of every paper something along the lines of, "There are grammar and usage mistakes as well, but they are not the concern at the moment." I did not think that misuse of personal pronouns, though vexing, was nearly as important as, say, a discontinuity in the way terms were used. Logical consistency is a huge aspect of any argument, and while all the papers summarily begged the reader for rather risky logical leaps, I primarily tried to show how to amend glaring logical errors.

My style of commenting leaves very little graphite in the margins, as I prefer to place my thoughts on a separate page. My feeling is that I cannot ask for clarity with vague, scribbled marginal notes. It is my responsibility to articulate exactly what I mean, and if that requires that I spend some time deliberating upon what I am going to say, all the better.

Fellowship of Motivation

I approached my conferences as an opportunity to establish trust with my students, to motivate them to write, and, lastly, to explain my typed comments. My reasoning was that unless I had the trust of the student, no suggestions or recommendations would truly be taken seriously. My feeling on motivation is that no demoralized student wants to do *anything*, and that I would have to put serious effort into making sure that students would leave our conference feeling *good* about their writing, rather than despondent at having a series of corrections. The explanation of my comments was somewhat extraneous. I typed the comments on a separate sheet so that we could spend more time discussing what to do rather than discerning what I meant.

I suppose that my conferences often took the form of Peter Elbow's comments. I sometimes was overenthusiastic about students' papers just to show that it wasn't a total uphill climb ahead. I spoke in terms of "we" so as to show that I saw the task at hand as a team effort. All of my comments went pretty well, as far as I'm concerned. All my students seemed receptive, with some of course being more vocal than others. It was during the conferences where I really got a grasp on where each student intended to go with his or her paper, and I felt genuine excitement when we could figure out a way to get there.

Fellowship of Improvement

There were logistical issues that I could not foresee when arranging certain elements of my first round. Next time, I will offer fewer time slots and place them earlier in the week. This way, I can use the tail end of the week for make-ups and rescheduling, as well as for second conferences. One of my students sent me a postconference second draft right before the paper was due. I looked it over, made a number of changes and suggestions, but ran out of time before we could actually get together and discuss the paper. This was frustrating, not just because I put a lot of extra work into something with no result, but because she really wanted to produce a good paper, and it's tough to see that kind of enthusiasm and miss an opportunity to work with it as much as possible.

I will gather telephone numbers and active email addresses from all my students. My first round was plagued by phone-tag and email games that resulted in two students who did not meet with me. I realize that it was their responsibility to contact me, but I wish that I would have been able to give them a call to find out what was going on.

The fellowship experience has been rather grueling to this point. It has been very difficult for me to balance the tutorship with my regular schoolwork and activities, but I feel that next round should be much easier to work with. Now that I understand the flow of things, I will be able to manage my time more wisely. I thoroughly enjoy working with other students—it's invigorating, really. Ironically, after prodding so many of them to construct viable conclusions to their papers, I myself am left with an open threshold to seal up. So, here goes [...]

In closing, *Webster's New Collegiate Dictionary* defines "conclusion" as "the last part of something," and, well, I agree. How's that for irony?

3

How to Conference and
Write Comments

The conferences were more productive than the written comments.

The written comments were meant to help me revise, but in the conference I could ask for a further explanation.

I liked the written comments because I could look them over when I had time.

—Comments from Student Surveys, La Salle University

Whether you are training to become a peer tutor in a writing center, where conferencing is the norm, or to become a Writing Fellow, you should be adept at both conferencing and writing comments on papers. In the writing center, for example, although you will spend most of your time conferencing, you may also write comments or summarize your suggestions for revision in writing. In a Writing Fellows program you may do both (write comments and conduct conferences with the same students), but sometimes you may not be able to meet with students, and you will need to respond to papers only through written comments, especially if you are working with students who take courses in the evenings or on weekends. (More on this in Chapter 6.)

In a study conducted by peer tutors at La Salle, "Student Perspectives on the Writing Fellows Program," the tutors found that most students say that comments and conferences are equally useful. However, as the student comments above indicate, some say conferences are more helpful whereas others learn more effectively from written comments. In an ideal world we would be able to tailor peer tutoring to the learning styles of our students. Although college is sometimes called the "ivory tower" (as opposed to the "real world"), I think you would agree that it is not an ideal world. Students may not get to choose the approach to peer tutoring which works best for them. Some schools have only a writing center where students are tutored through conferencing and other students find themselves in a Writing Fellows-assisted class where they may receive only written comments if they can't attend conferences.

Conferences

Because writing centers are far more numerous than Writing Fellows programs, the conference is still the primary model for tutoring in writing. In a few years, perhaps, I may need to revise that statement, not because of a huge growth in Writing Fellow programs, but because of the increasing influence of technology in education. However, just as distance learning, despite predictions to the contrary, has not made the classroom teacher obsolete, online tutoring will most likely never replace the writing conference. The one-on-one conference is personal. I like the way Walvoord discusses the benefits of conferences:

> [You] read the paper in the student's presence and share your pleasure at success and your suggestions for improvement. You watch each other's expressions and get past the coldness of red ink and into the warmth of person meeting person [. . .] you encourage students to take responsibility for conducting and planning their own work [. . .] A student's paper, like a child's drawing is a gift, a self-revelation, an act of communication; the conference provides a rich opportunity to respond to it at that level. (144)

Here are just some of the topics treated in the literature on conferencing:

- What is the benefit of the conference in contrast to written comments?
- What is the more effective approach to use when conferencing—asking questions or giving suggestions?
- What kinds of questions and comments are most effective?
- How long should conferences be?
- How long should you wait when there is silence during the conference?

- How much writing should take place during the conference and in what form?
- Who should do the writing?
- If you comment on the draft beforehand and then see the student in a follow up conference, what is the role of the conference vis-à-vis the written comments?

This chapter will suggest possible answers to these questions.

The Theory

The growth of writing centers had led to an extensive literature on conferencing. Whole books are devoted to the subject (for example *Training Tutors for Writing Conferences, The Dynamics of The Writing Conference, Teaching One-to-One, A Tutor's Guide: Helping Writers One to One*). Articles on conferencing by teachers and peer tutors appear frequently in the *Writing Center Journal* and the *Writing Lab Newsletter*. I reviewed some of the theory and research on conferencing in Chapter 1.

Most accepted conference practice is based on the major theories which drove the revolution in teaching composition also discussed in Chapter 1: theories which used the needs of the student as a starting point in education, rather than the subject matter they study, theories which advocate self-expression as an important learning goal, and theories explaining how students learn to write, specifically cognitive and the social constructionist theories. The conference is a form of individualizing education; the conference promotes self-expression; cognitive theories of learning support writing drafts, and social constructionism validates conferencing where tutor and student engage in a dialogue that is in itself a model of academic discourse.

While most experts in the field favor the nondirective form of conferencing, some scholars have questioned a "blind adherence to non-directive tutoring practices based on the social constructionist theories" (Carino 96). Carino reviews the work of those scholars who have begun to think about power and authority as reference points for describing the peer tutor's role. He adds, "to pretend that there is not a hierarchical relationship between tutor and student is a fallacy, and to divest the tutor of power and authority at times is foolish and may even be unethical" (98). Carino notes that the nondirective model, while still the most popular basis for conducting conferences, has been challenged by scholars like John Trimbur in "Peer Tutoring: A Contradiction in Terms" who questions the notion of peerness given the unequal positions of tutor and tutee.

Carino and others suggest that a reciprocal dialogue is not always possible, especially with some students. For example, here is a situation where the student lacks knowledge, but the tutor still tries to be nondirective:

TUTOR.   After reading through your paper, I am wondering why you spent the first page writing about what you and your friends did on the way to the theatre.

STUDENT.   I don't know. That's what happened. We met in town, then drove to campus, and had a hard time finding a parking space, like I said.

TUTOR.   Well, do you think that it is important for the reader to know?

STUDENT.   Well, I thought I would put it in to get started and I thought it was neat the way we got lucky and got a space just when we thought we'd be late. I wanted to start with something interesting, and I thought the play was serious, heavy.

TUTOR.   It is interesting, but how do you see it relating to the play?

STUDENT.   I don't know. Should I take it out?

TUTOR.   What do you think?

Here is the more directive version of the conference:

TUTOR.   After reading your paper, I see you have a long part about getting to the theatre. Have you ever written a play review before?

STUDENT.   No, I put that in because I thought it was interesting the way we got a parking space the last minute. I wanted to start with something interesting before doing all the stuff about the play, which I thought was really serious, heavy.

TUTOR.   Yes, it's good to start with something interesting, but did your teacher explain anything about how to write the review?

STUDENT.   No, we just had a little sheet I gave you saying we had to write the review, how many pages, and when the play is on.

TUTOR.   Well, in a play review, you might have a short introduction, where you should start as close to the play as possible because your purpose is to help the reader decide if they want to see the play or not. You need to cut the part about getting to the theatre and start with a sentence where you say, "*Oleanna* is a play that will make people think." That is a short direct sentence, and it previews what follows (Carino 105–106).

These two short conference scripts are a good example of a situation in which the tutor should be more forthcoming. It's impossible for the student to participate actively because he is not aware of the conventions of the play review.

Flexibility: The "Mantra" of Good Conferences

Most composition experts agree that peer conferences should be a collaborative activity during which the tutor and student work together to improve the paper. Although there is considerable consensus as to how to accomplish this aim, the variables that affect conferencing require tutors to be flexible. Personal meetings involve feelings as well as the intellect. If a student is anxious, you probably need to change your game plan. Also, remember that students will often arrive at the writing center with particular expectations about the role of the peer tutor. You may find it difficult to get them to collaborate, and then you will switch to more directive tutoring.

The suggestions below (adapted from the guidelines for conferencing in *Training Tutors for Writing Conferences* and *The Bedford Guide to Peer Tutoring*) will help you get started. Once you are familiar with them, you can try adapting them to different tutoring situations. Eventually, you will need to find your own style of conferencing—what works best for you, given your personality, the way you interact with people, and the students you tutor.

Preparations

Preparing (or not preparing) for the writing conference can make or break the conference. Writing conferences should be conducted in a relatively quiet place with few distractions. If you are lucky, your campus will have a designated place for student conferences, such as a writing center with appropriate conference stations that are relatively private. You may even have the use of a computer. However, many campuses are short on space. At La Salle, we do have a writing center, but all of our tutoring sessions cannot be accommodated there. I urge peer tutors to reserve study group rooms in the library or in another location that is easy to find, such as seminar class rooms, which are not in use during the free periods. If space is a problem on your campus, in addition to telling the students where you will meet them, post the conference location in an obvious place, such as the library bulletin board.

Arrange the conference situation so that you sit side by side with the writer, rather than across from each other. This arrangement makes you seem less authoritarian and permits you and the student to look at the paper together. If you are working with a computer, let the student sit in front of it and control the keyboard. This placement reinforces the idea that the paper is the student's work, not yours.

Be sure to have a pen, a pad, a composition handbook, and a dictionary nearby. The student should do most of the writing, but you may occasionally want to demonstrate a point or summarize the discussion. It would be best if you write on a note pad; the student should do the writing on his paper. A handbook and a dictionary can be helpful for clarifying a rule of grammar or punctuation or checking an ambiguous spelling.

Scheduling suggestions

Try not to schedule conferences back to back. Make sure that there is a 10-minute interval between conferences. You don't want the student you are tutoring to feel rushed, but you also want to avoid having students wait. Sometimes the hallway in the English Department looks like the waiting room in a doctor's office!

Regarding the length of conferences, many writing centers use 30 minutes as a guide. It's the rare student who can tolerate talking about his or her paper for more than 30 minutes, although there are exceptions. Some students will indicate by their body language or their comments that 15 to 20 minutes is all they can handle. Once students are familiar with the writing center, and more comfortable with the tutoring situation, they may be able to work with you for as long as an hour, especially those students who come to the writing center frequently. As students begin to feel more comfortable in the writing center, they will participate more actively in their conferences.

The tutoring session

Begin the conference by getting acquainted. (Remember the discussion in Chapter 2.) Then find out the student's reason for coming to the writing center and find out all you can about the writing assignment. You may want to begin by addressing the student's concerns first if he is able to express them. That is not always the case. The student may simply say, "I know this draft is not good. I always have trouble with literature papers." If that's the case then begin by addressing issues which affect the whole paper, such as making sure that it conforms to the assignment instructions, and that the ideas are logically organized and developed sufficiently (often called Higher Order Concerns), prior to discussing sentence level concerns (Lower Order Concerns). But no rule is hard and fast. If the paper is riddled with many sentence level errors, you may want to begin by discussing them first. Some instructors will simply stop reading these papers and give them a failing grade.

You have three powerful tools at your disposal to tackle these problems: "active listening, facilitating by responding as a reader, and silence and wait time to allow a writer to think" (Ryan 16). Sit next to the writer and read along silently as the writer reads the paper aloud. Encourage the writer to tell you what he or she wants the two of you to look and listen for. Ask the writer the following questions at this stage:

- What works best in your paper?
- What do you like best or feel most satisfied about?
- What works least in the paper?
- Which parts did you have trouble writing?
- Which parts don't feel right?

These are open-ended questions. They are

> broad in scope and require more than a few words of response. They help you to learn more about a writer's attitudes, the writer's specific problems with writing or writing assignments, and the writer's expectations. On the other hand, questions such as "Do you have some ideas for that section?" require a yes or no answer or brief limited response. These questions can elicit specific information about the paper. (Ryan 18)

Both kinds of questions are useful. In either case, count to five silently after asking a question. Dr. Dell Hymes, a linguistic anthropologist and one of my favorite professors, says that Americans have a problem with silence; it makes us nervous. We always think we know the answers and find it hard to give someone else the opportunity to discover the answers for himself or herself. Silence is what the student who is trying to think needs most. My own children are always chiding me for interrupting them or finishing their sentences!

Here is Leigh Ryan's suggestion for overcoming this problem:

> Try this experiment. Get a watch or a clock with a second hand. At the start of a minute turn around and place the clock out of sight. When you think that a minute has elapsed, look back. How close did you come? Thirty seconds? Forty-five? Chances are you stopped too soon. And that is what we tend to do, when we try making ourselves wait; we jump in a little too soon. (21)

Give the writer a chance to solve a problem before you offer specific solutions. Your task is to help the writers see the problem and solve it themselves, if possible. Avoid jumping in and writing out the solution yourself. Let the writer do the writing. Eric DePaul, a La Salle tutor, learned this skill during his first semester of tutoring writing:

> I learned when to keep speaking and when to remain silent. Some of the students were more talkative than others, and I discovered that the more conversational types usually were more likely to share their ideas with me. I found that if I aimed these students on the right track in our conversation, they would proceed to offer an idea or two that they had, as so long as I continued prompting them, they would continue on the correct path. On the other side of the token, I found that I would sometimes offer information that the student would need a minute or two to think about. When I simply had the feeling that he/she needed a moment to think, I found that it was best to remain silent at this point and give the student a few moments to contemplate. In the end, I discovered that it was much easier to know when I should prompt a student than when I should remain silent.

Concluding the tutoring session

Be sure to summarize the ideas for revision that you discussed during the conference, either verbally or both verbally and in writing. For example, you might say, "So, let's see, you plan to rewrite the introduction," and so on. Also, ask the students if they have additional questions. Remind the students that they can return to the writing center with another draft if they have time before the paper is due. Be friendly as you say "good-bye." Some tutors give students their phone numbers and email addresses just in case the students want to get in touch. One appreciative student at La Salle had this to say about her tutor: "Stacey was very helpful. She even emailed me after a conference to follow up on something she was unsure of!"

When the writer comes without a complete draft

If the writer can't get started on the assignment, then try to find out why. There are several possibilities. Sometimes the writer doesn't understand the assignment. On the other hand, the assignment may not be the problem, but the writer may have "writer's block"; he becomes paralyzed when he is given any writing assignment. In the first case, you should review the assignment with the writer. Kelly Tierney, a La Salle tutor, reports that students were grateful for help understanding the assignment. She says, "After each conference, most of the students thanked me. As they left the conference, the freshmen told me that I was a big help, since most of them did not know what the teacher expected from a paper. Numerous students asked me questions about papers they had to write for other courses."

In the second case, when the student "freezes" at the sight of a writing assignment, you should discuss strategies for getting started, such as making lists or experimenting with free writing (writing without editing). Once the student realizes that he or she, in fact, has something to say about the topic, some of the stress may disappear. Another approach involves structured questioning. For example, if the topic is to write a character analysis of a short story, you might ask, "Who is the main character? What is his problem? Does he solve it? If so, how?" Many composition handbooks include questions relevant to different kinds of topics. You may want to consult your trusty handbook if you need some help developing questions. The student plagued with writing anxiety will probably need to be seen during both the planning and revising stage of writing the paper. You might suggest meeting again once he has some ideas written down. (More about this topic in Chapter 5.)

Then there is the student who does not have a writing problem, but cannot get started because he or she in fact has a reading problem. Judy Trachtenberg, a reading specialist who tutored in our writing center for many years, says that some students have difficulty reading the materials necessary for writing their papers. These texts range from primary texts to fiction to their own textbooks. I often find this to be the case in literature courses. For example, when I asked the students in one of my literature courses to explain what they find most difficult about writing papers, overwhelmingly they responded that they were not sure they understood the short stories or novels we were reading using the traditional tools of literary analysis taught in literature courses. Here are some of their comments:

> When we are assigned a paper to write in a literature class we are often asked to identify themes in the writing. This aspect is difficult for me perhaps because I am unclear on what exactly a theme is. (Diane Kovac)

> The most difficult part of writing literature papers is that it is difficult sometimes to understand the story or different aspects of it that you are trying to write about. It doesn't matter how well you write or how well you can say something if you don't understand what you are trying to say or what you are supposed to say. (Tracy Loh)

> I feel it is difficult writing papers literature classes because there are so many different interpretations for one story that I am afraid my interpretation is incorrect. (Christina Ziccardi)

As you see from these students' comments, it's possible that the student who thinks he cannot read the material is often blocked by a fear of giving the wrong answer. By discussing the material with the student, you may help him or her to overcome this fear, or, if he or she does not understand the material, then you may be able to help him or her understand the text by suggesting that the student bring it to the next session to review together.

Conferencing after commenting in writing

If you have read the draft beforehand, as you will if you are assigned to a class as a Writing Fellow, you will need to distinguish between the role of the conference and the role of your written comments. Those of us who direct Writing Fellows programs see this situation as ideal; the tutor responds twice to the student, once in writing and once in person. Try to capitalize on the particular advantage of each of these response modes. Here are some hints:

- Use the conference to review your written comments to be sure that the student understands them.
- Focus on one or two problems you identified in your written comments, and try to help the student solve them.
- Find out how the student feels about this assignment and writing papers in general.

Many of the students who have the assistance of a Writing Fellow report that conferences and comments are equally useful. One member of a class where the students did not meet with the Writing Fellow but only received written comments wrote on the student survey distributed at the end of the semester: "Make sure that the students meet with the Writing Fellow instead of just handing back checked papers in class." In response to the question, "In what ways could written comments have been more useful to you?" the same student said, "If we met and went over the comments." In response to the question "How many conferences would you like to have had?" one student wrote, "As many as were needed to get my papers to where they should have been." Students seem to like the personal touch.

Writing tutors personalities and their conferences

No two writing conferences are alike, because no two peer tutors or tutees are alike. These comments below by two writing tutors demonstrate that the peer tutor's personality plays an important role in shaping the conference. Steve Martin, a "let's get down to business" person, likes structure. On the other hand, Mary Therese Motley is more "laid back." Notice how they begin their conferences:

Steve Martin:

I began each conference with the same three questions: Is there anything Dr. X pointed out in your last paper that you feel you need to address in this one? Is there anything that you struggled to express in your paper that you feel I may be of help with? Is there anything in particular you would like to focus on in this conference? One student who had difficulty matching up his conclusions with his thesis in the first paper asked that we go over what Dr. X had pointed out. These questions helped ground the conference from the very beginning.

Mary Therese K. Motley:

When students arrived I introduced myself and tried to make them feel comfortable. In a few cases, students were very receptive and seemed to really think about what I was telling them. They asked questions and tried some new sentences or ideas for organization. One meeting went well past the allotted twenty minutes as I tried to explain the citation format and consistent use of tenses. Eventually she seemed to understand what I was saying, but I loaned her my Pocket Reference for Writers handbook and hoped that that would clear up any further questions.

Additional comments by Mary Therese demonstrate that writing tutors must be flexible. Students, like peer tutors, are not all the same:

Conversely I had a few conferences that were maybe seven minutes long. During one meeting I felt like I was sitting next to the model student for Muriel Harris' article about the unresponsive student. The girl came in, told me that she had not spent much time on her draft so she knew it needed work, and proceeded to remain silent for the rest of the time, despite my attempts to engage her in conversation. I went through some of the main problems with her paper and asked if she had any question; she shook her head "no" and promptly left. What did surprise me was that students who did not have many problems were the most concerned about their drafts and had the longest conferences. Perhaps students who are already good writers and have had many experiences writing are the ones most interested in improving upon their work.

Common Problems
"No Shows" and reluctant writers
"No shows" are a problem. There you are, awaiting your tutees. You have carefully worked out your own schedule in order to work in the writing center. Students have signed up for appointments. The first one

does not appear. Admittedly you have other things you can do to pass the time, but you are disappointed. You are not alone—your teachers face this problem all the time. There is not much you can do when a student does not show up. You might try to reduce the number of "no shows" by sending your tutees email reminders a day or two before their appointments. But, I don't advocate chasing them down. That's not your job. However, it is important for you to take "no shows" in stride and not permit your disappointment to undermine your other conferences.

Perhaps even more frustrating is the student who does indeed appear but remains passive throughout the conference. Muriel Harris' essay, "Talk to Me: Engaging Reluctant Writers," is an excellent summary of the reasons students are not responsive at writing conferences. She offers some very sound suggestions for dealing with these students. As with the paper which we think has been carelessly written, we can only guess as to the reasons students will not participate actively in the conference setting: The student is forced to be there; writing is not important to this writer; the writer may be anxious about revealing her ignorance or poor writing; the writer is overwhelmed with other concerns; the writer doesn't have the language to talk about writing; the writer is simply a quiet person; the writer knows if he shuts up the tutor will do all the work. Here are some of Harris' recommendations for dealing with the "reluctant writer." (The suggestions are hers; I've summarized them and added examples from my own experiences.)

Empathize with the student

Let the students know that you too have been in the same position—having to accomplish some task in college which you didn't relish. For example, I always tell my students about how difficult it was for me to pass college courses in history. In my case, I forced myself to sit in the library every Sunday to memorize the dates of important events.

Acknowledge the students' lack of interest in writing

If the student says something like "I hate to write," you might respond, "Well, OK, but the fact that you came to the writing center for help means that you want to get a decent grade on this paper, right? So let's start working."

Help the student talk about his or her fears

When the student says, "I'm a terrible writer," I usually say, "I wish I had a dollar for every student who makes that statement." You, as a tutor, might say, "I have learned in my peer tutoring course that few people, not just students, think they are good writers. However, I also learned that writing well is something that everyone of average intelligence can do (as opposed to becoming a great artist, for example)." Then remind the student that your job is not to criticize, but to help. Most students who say "I am a terrible writer" are terribly afraid of criticism.

Reschedule for a better time or listen and move on

Some students are preoccupied with more serious problems than their essay when they are scheduled for a conference, even when they themselves have set up the conference. If a student seems very distracted, you might ask if there is something else more pressing right now. If their answer is yes, recommend that they reschedule (Harris 28–29) and, perhaps, visit the counseling center. Be cautious when taking this approach. You are not a counselor.

Written Comments

Many of the same principles we discussed about conferencing apply to written comments as well, but you need to try even harder to avoid sounding like a teacher when commenting in writing. The temptation to imitate the comments you have received on your own papers is very great. Remember our discussion in Chapter 2 about sounding like a tutor, not a teacher. We stressed using qualifiers (for example "I *think* (the qualifier) your introduction is effective") and sounding personal ("As I read your paper it reminded me of [...]") but the discussion doesn't end there. For example, if you are tutoring in a Writing Fellows program, think about these questions when writing comments on papers:

- How long should my summary comment be?
- Are comments in the margin more effective than comments at the end of the paper?
- Are interlinear (comments between the lines) comments effective or distracting?
- Is it more effective to write directly on the student paper or to attach your comments on a separate sheet?

Unfortunately (or fortunately!) there is no magic formula for writing comments. Think back to the kinds of comments by your teachers that were helpful. Try to use them as a model for your comments. But here is another hint—keep an index card on your desk, which says: **My purpose is to help this student revise the paper, not to rewrite the paper for him**.

The End Comment (also called Summary Comment)

To respond to the paper as a reader would, you must give your general impression of the paper. When you write end comments, begin with the positive (when possible) and then point out the most serious problem in the paper. For example, if the student has not answered the assignment question, then start there. Here's what you might say, about a paper on characterization in the novel *The Accidental Tourist* by Anne Tyler, "I enjoyed your essay on *The Accidental Tourist*, a favorite novel of mine. I especially liked the section about Macon Leary, the main character. However, I think you need to reread the assignment. Notice that the instructions indicate that you should also write about Muriel and Alexander, in addition to Macon. Also, I wasn't sure why you wrote about Macon's problems with his dog Edward first."

The following excerpt is from the beginning of a paper written in response to an assignment in a course in community health nursing. The assignment required students to write a summary of the contents of the first four weeks of the course for the purpose of informing a nursing student unfamiliar with the course materials. The writer organizes the report chronologically in terms of the material in each lecture. Notice the Writing Fellows summary comment which appears after the paper: It begins positively and then is limited to the major problem in the paper—the way the material in the paper is organized.

Sample student paper: Introduction

With the beginning of class the course syllabus and course requirements were reviewed. I found there to be special import on the necessity of completing all the readings.

We began by discussing the ANA newsletter that is a position paper on the definition and role of public health nursing in the delivery of health care. The topic was to be continued later. There seemed to be too much class discussion at this point.

Seeing different parts of the population as aggregates was also a high priority of this lecture, and linked with this was the recognition of the health care need outside an institutional framework, yet without labeling the nurse that functions in this area as having a specialty. Also, in this session we were introduced to the Environmental Health Model.

Tutor's comment

Dear Student,

Your essay seems to include much of the information taught during the first four weeks of class. However, a student who is not in the class will want to know which material was emphasized and how the major themes of the content were organized, rather than what was covered in each section. A summary usually includes these characteristics. Try to organize the paper according to the logic of the content, rather than give a blow-by-blow account of each lecture. And [...] in the margins I made some notes to help you make some of your sentences more effective.

As to length, there is no evidence as to whether longer or shorter comments are more effective. But, for sure, a two-line summary comment for a five-page paper is too short, and a two-page comment written in response to a one-page paper is too long. Here is a paper that could have been written in a philosophy class. The summary comment is clearly too long. Read the paper and the peer tutor's comment. Then write your own comment.

Sample student paper

It is said that humans' only motivation is self-interest. There are many things that can be said about this. First of all you could bring up such people as Mother Teresa; someone who obviously gave everything she had, physical and emotional, to others. Then, however, the backers of this self-interest philosophy would only comment in saying that the said "good" person is merely doing these good deeds in order to better their own self later on in another life or something similar.

Technically, however, they cannot read minds and therefore do not know if people's intentions are purely innocent and generous or not. On the other hand, we also do not know people's thoughts, so that is why the controversy is so great.

It is easy for these people to promote the idea of total self-interest. They say that everyone does things for their own gain. They merely say that people go about pursuing this using different means. They offer such suggestions as the pursuit of pleasure, power, wealth, and/or status. That makes it a lot easier for them to pin this supposed motivation on everyone in the human race. By doing that they're leaving nowhere for people to turn, while also offering no unquestionable evidence. They even attack the meek and timid, saying that these people attempt to get others to like them and seek their approval.

What these people seem to be doing, ultimately, is making up excuses. They accuse the human race of being doomed into only looking out for themselves, so we might as well not even try. It is merely giving up. The real test for people is to overcome.

Tutor's summary comment

Dear Student X:

You approach this paper with an argument against the logic of the self-interest position. Any time one argues against a stance on logical grounds, the demands increase. You present the idea that the self-interest position is ultimately incoherent. Your ability to pick out hidden inconsistencies and exploit them is truly a skill. We will work this paper so that it clearly depicts the problems you have with the assertions in question. In order to do this, I will go over what I gathered from your paper.

It seems that you want to say the following: To know the motivation of any behavior is a somewhat suspect task. Motive refers to the mental conditions that provoked the behavior in question. There is a glaring weakness in any argument for motivation after the fact. All explanation of motivation can be shaped to fit the theory of self-interest. I thought of this example and thought that it rings with what you are pointing out. If I say that all humans love gerbils, and that all human behavior is motivated by the urge to do something nice for gerbils, then all behavior can be retrospectively judged to fit this pattern. One could say that Mother Theresa most certainly did not feed the hungry for the sake of gerbils, and I would say, "Oh yes she did. Because all behavior is motivated by love of gerbils, then Mother Theresa must believe that gerbils would somehow benefit from feeding the poor of Calcutta." This analogy seems odd, and I hope it doesn't confuse you, but your analysis of the emptiness and ultimate failure of the argument is highly sophisticated. You use the term *excuses*, claiming that it leaves no response that could not be distorted by the self-interest position. I think you are arguing that the argument is merely a neat trick.

It is important to note that some human behavior is motivated by self-interest, and you do concede while making the careful observation that occasional self-absorption does not require self-interest as the motive for all behavior. Again, you are arguing that the logical leap that the self-interest stance asks is too much.

I think what we want to do is frame an outline at the conference. Your paper is highly directed and specific, it attacks two logical problems you have with the position: To say that self-interest is the sole motivator is incorrect because it relies on the judgment of mental conditions that we cannot know. Attributing all action to self-interest is nothing more than excuse making. Self-absorption does not mean that all behavior is self-interest based. We want to use these points to create a strong and clear thesis, and frame the paper using these points. See you at the conference!

Steve Martin

Comments in the Margin

The advantage of comments in the margin is that they are next to sections that are the subject of the comments. I like Walvoord's description of the role of comments in the margin: "They may illustrate a point that is stated more generally at the end" [...] or "marginal comments may also point out matters that are specific to a spot in the text and are not included in the summary comment." She warns, "Be careful not to make marginal comments that imply that the text merely needs clearing up for punctuation and diction, when your summary comment implies that the student needs to make major changes" (142).

If you use marginal comments to note problems in sentences, be sure to refer to them in the end comment. For example, in the summary comment you might say, "After you have reviewed the organization of your ideas, you should edit for punctuation errors. I was very distracted by them when reading your paper."

Be sure that your comments in the margin are written clearly. A scribbled unintelligible comment is no comment at all. I've written my share of these. When students approach the desk, after I have returned a set of papers, with that puzzled look, I know that it's for one of two reasons. They are disappointed about their grade, or they can't decipher my handwriting. Even more embarrassing are the times when even I can't understand my own handwriting!

Avoid terse comments such as *awkward* or *unclear* or *lacks development*. At some level these statements could be classified as readerly comments. They do in fact express your reactions to the text. However, students rarely understand them. What may sound awkward or unclear to you may sound just fine to the student. Instead you might say, "I'm not sure this is the best word for what I think you mean." Some sentences seem awkward because the syntax is problematic. For example, if a student wrote, "I found there to be special import on the necessity of completing all readings," I would have been inclined to write "awk" in my earlier days of teaching composition. Then my students would say, "That sentence doesn't sound awkward to me." Sometimes it helps to work back from your own revision of the sentence, which you don't show to the student. For example, I would revise this sentence to say, "The teacher made it clear that we were to complete all the readings." Then I would say to the student, "This sentence doesn't sound right to me. Maybe starting with 'The teacher said [...]' might make it sound better." Starting sentences with the subject, the person who commits the action, has miraculous effects on "awkward" sentences. (More about this in Chapter 4.)

"Development" is also a moving target. For example, students will ask, "Do you mean I need another sentence?" Instead of "lacks development" say (remembering Walvoord's second- and third-level response guidelines) "I don't understand this point. Can you give an example from your recent experiences?"

Regarding interlinear comments (comments written between the lines); avoid the impulse to cross out the "wrong" word and replace it with a better one or to correct punctuation errors. I confess that I am guilty of both of these practices. You will find that you are in constant battle with yourself to suppress the inclination to edit the paper. (Remember that part of the index card warning: "avoid rewriting the paper.") Circling the wrong word, or underlining it is a better approach. You can do the same with punctuation problems and then explain your symbols (for example circling, underlining) in the end comment with statements such as, "I've underlined words which I think you should reconsider, and I have circled commas which I think are unnecessary."

The comments in the margin to a paper that could have been written in response to an assignment in a course in religion by Writing Fellow Victoria Franz are good examples of the readerly approach to comments in the margin. Also, notice her reference to the comments in the margin in her summary comment.

Sample student paper

"Morality: An Ever-Present and Ever-Changing Issue in Our Society"

Morality is a concept that is interpreted differently among various groups, depending upon culture, and background. Broadly speaking, morality is essentially a set of standards and guidelines by which one chooses to live his or her life. It is how we perceive the things that are going on around us, and, in turn, how we respond to those actions and to the people involved in them. It is essentially a universal principle, but it is altered as far as its composition and importance by other outside factors, such as one's religion, cultural background, and beliefs.

Regardless, every person has their own set of morals and values that heavily influence the decisions that they make and the way that they choose to live their lives.

Morality can be derived from various different sources, and a person's moral code is determined by which of those sources they hold as most important. A very spiritual person may adept their morals from their religious beliefs and education whereas a person without such religious convictions may develop their morals based solely on their upbringing and what they perceive in the world around them. To varying degrees, religious upbringing, the media, culture and a whole slew of other factors contribute to one's perception of morality and acceptable moral behavior.

The importance of morality is also a very subjective matter. As a whole, our society holds morality as being a very important part of our everyday lives. However, if we look beyond the aggregate picture and begin to examine people on an individual basis, we see that not everyone places the same high value on morality. It is those people with a low opinion of the importance of morality that cause problems in our society. Often times these are people who are not religious, that had a poor upbringing, that were not brought up with a certain level of respect for dignity and the value of human life. (Gilmore, 3)

These ideas provide an introduction into the next issue: the decline of morality in our society. Although our society holds morality in high regard, it doesn't seem to be as important as it has been in the past. As society progresses (or digresses, depending on your perspective), things that were once considered outlandish and offensive are now becoming more socially acceptable and prevalent in today's society. Some people are disturbed or frightened by this. As a result, people can become hypocritical when evaluating their moral position. As the old adage states, "Actions speak louder than words." These people declare their moral standards and state that they are opposed to some of the things going on around them, but their actions do not reflect those beliefs. The reasoning behind this is that society is changing, and the general tendency seems to be for morals to conform to society rather than for society to change based upon moral convictions. Thus, although these people carry these high moral values, they are forced to sacrifice their position in order to function as "normal" members of society.

> Very insightful!

> Like What?

> Are these people the same ones you were talking about?

As demonstrated by other points previously presented. In this essay, moral standards are quite conditional. As a whole, there are some standards that our society holds to be universal (value of human life, etc.). but even those standards are not applicable to each individual person.

> Transition should be stronger

American society today is melting pot of world cultures, and to attempt to standardize and codify a universal set of morals are to rob this society of its diversity and uniqueness. Each person is entitled to his or her own beliefs, be they religious and moral. With people coming from such diverse religious, cultural, and ethical backgrounds, it is impossible to have a universal code of morals by which every person in our ever-changing society is going to live their life. Overall, morals are important, but each and every person is entitled to their own set of morals and to choose what role those morals will *play* in the choices that they make and the lives that they lead.

Tutor's summary comment

It's quite obvious that you have given issues of morality a lot of thought. I like how your main point, that morality is universal, but mostly subjective, is addressed in every part of the paper—it makes the paper flow nicely. (which is perhaps why I was disappointed as a reader by some of your transitions. I have marked them.) I think, however, you need to clarify your discussion of universal vs. conditional. You start the paper saying that morality is both, but you end very passionately claiming that it is impossible to have a universal code of morality (I know what you mean, but I think you should explain further).

Also, your discussion of the importance of morality starts out strong, but I felt that you should talk more about it. (This was one of the four questions of the assignment.) A lot of what I underlined was the annoying subject–verb agreement stuff. You can't say "person" (singular) and then "their lives" (plural). I know it's annoying, but you should go back and find ways to change these. Overall, I really liked your paper!

Vicki

Writing Comments on the Student's Paper/Attaching Comments/Using a Checklist Form

As with all pedagogical choices, whatever you do has benefits and limitations. Writing the summary comment on the student's paper, either on the bottom of the last page or on the back of the paper, gives you the freedom to read papers wherever you are—on the train, in the library, and so on. All you need is a pen or pencil. However, there are two main disadvantages to this approach:

1. The student cannot read the comment and the paper side by side, since the comment is usually on the bottom of the last page.
2. The student may have difficulty understanding your comment if your handwriting is poor.

A third possible objection to writing on students' papers: students may see this practice as a violation of their papers. You have marred their creation. However, in all my years of teaching I have never met a student who felt that way. Most students seem very grateful for a response that is longer than "Good job" or "Poorly written." The fourth disadvantage is real. If you write on students' papers, you cannot easily revise your comments, unless you use pencil. At times you may want to rewrite your comments. For example, as a result of reading the other students' papers, you may revise your judgment of the paper. Or you may simply feel your comments are too negative or not sufficiently clear. Especially during your first tutoring experiences, you may be somewhat indecisive when you write comments.

Attaching a sheet with your summary comment has several advantages: You can discard your comment with a flick of the staple remover, if you change your mind. Also, you can type your comments, which can speed up the process. However, beware! You may find yourself writing very long comments because of the ease of typing. Remember, your comment shouldn't be longer than the student's paper!

Checklists

Checklists, which include a list of your criteria for evaluating the paper, have several advantages. When you use a checklist you are more likely to respond to all aspects of the paper. Also, checklists can help students understand responses that appear in outline form with headings. However (surprise, surprise!), checklists also have disadvantages. You may sound more like a teacher and less like a tutor when you "fill in the blanks" on a checklist. And the order of your comments will be dictated by the checklist rather than your own sense of what's most important. For example, the tutor who used the checklist shown in p. 62 wrote to the student: "You successfully answered the question," before giving his or her reaction to the paper. He or she might have begun by saying, "I enjoyed your paper." It was very informative if he or she had written a summary comment. Also, a checklist forces us to speak in generalities rather than address the specifics of the paper. Be careful to write complete sentences if you decide to try out this mode of response and address the specifics of the paper. Eric DePaul, who was a tutor in the Writing Fellows program, thinks the checklist is a good idea:

> I think the checklist is beneficial to the student because it presents commentary in such an orderly fashion. When students view the checklist, they can easily discover what are the strengths and weaknesses of their papers, as the

checklist presents separate sections of commentary for the paper's focus, the organization, the development, the style of writing, and the sentence structure. When writing comments on the checklist sheets, I tried to follow the same basic rules that I attempted to utilize in my marginal comments, those rules being careful wording, specificity, and avoidance of repetition. Moreover, I found that I had to be even more conscientious in writing comments on the checklist since being both specific and non-repetitive was more difficult as I was dealing with more general areas of concern and had already offered significant commentary. I also used the checklist sheet to offer praise when appropriate.

The checklist in p. 62 has been used by writing tutors who want to experiment with this form of response. Notice how it can be used to respond to a paper that could have been written in response to this assignment in a course in philosophy.

The assignment (Marc Moreau, Instructor)

Your assignment is to compose an essay that answers the following questions: Can any of Aristotle's three categories—incontinence, intemperance, or disease—be appropriately applied to former President Clinton or to Monica Lewinsky on account of their admitted sexual relationship? What is the significance of your answer to the preceding question?

Sample student paper

The concepts of incontinence and intemperance are interesting to compare. They are also very relevant in relation to our society. Some would argue that incontinence is the more innocent of the two, while others say that this leads to intemperance. I definitely believe that Aristotle's ideas pertaining to incontinence, intemperance, and disease apply to President Clinton and most of the human race for that matter. We are all aware of what President Clinton did. Because of his actions the American people have no respect for the man because of his lack of morality.

It is my belief that one must look deeper than to simply say that he is a bad person because President: Clinton succumbed to temptation. At first he engaged in incontinence, and then it developed into intemperance. The distinction one must make is at what point do we feel guilt or shame about what we have done? Many people experience incontinence daily. It is up to the individual to decide when to discontinue the act so that it does not develop into intemperance.

As far as disease is concerned, Clinton might be a nymphomaniac. I agree that there could be a possible problem in his personality. If it is as such, then we as a people should recognize his need for rehabilitation. We should not shun the man. I find it very interesting that Aristotle lived so long ago and that his work has transcended time. He understood about these mental issues. He understood that it takes an entire lifetime to become wise. I agree with Aristotle when he says that that these vices flaw the human character. Do we bring them upon ourselves, or are they just there?

Monica on the other hand has a different type of problem. She engaged in sexual acts with the President, but I do not believe that incontinence or intemperance apply as much here to her. Her motives were not purely physical. She suffers from extremely low self-esteem and it should be recognized as such. It even goes deeper than that. She was looking for someone to make her feel special. I truly believe that Monica was in love with the President, where as it was purely physical for him. Monica craved attention. She is a young girl who is so insecure about herself. She needs help. Not our scorn. What the two did was morally wrong in context. But who are we to judge another? I know that I am not perfect. Incontinence and intemperance are daily issues for most people. We are all weak; it is in our human nature. We have to understand these weaknesses and offer rehabilitation.

Here is a sample checklist response to the paper. (Which comments are most helpful? Which comments could be improved?)

The checklist

Strengths: You successfully answered the question of the assignment and structured the paper so that it is clear to read.

Clarity of focus: I think you should introduce the book and both of your subjects in the introduction. Your conclusion was confusing to me and I think the focus of the paper was lost here.

Effectiveness of organization: The organization if fine, but the information you give in paragraph 3 seems out of place. Perhaps the analysis of Aristotle should go in the conclusion.

Effectiveness of the argument: You can develop your analysis of the former president and Monica. Explain how their actions have put them in these categories. Also, please use quotes from the text. They will support your thesis.

Appropriateness of style: Your sentences seem choppy at times— especially toward the bottom of page 2. I suggest you combine some of the sentences for more complex sentences.

Correctness: Grammar, Punctuation, and Spelling: Please use spell check before handing in the paper. You have some other minor grammatical errors, which I identified in your paper.

You may want to experiment with checklists. Sometimes when they first start tutoring, tutors like using checklists. When they gain more confidence in their tutoring skills, they often find that a checklist is inhibiting.

Common Problems

A major dilemma often confronting tutors who read drafts prior to seeing students is the suspicion that they are reading a draft written 10 minutes before the draft was due. What to do? You are very suspicious, but you cannot be sure. In the days when papers were handwritten, we could detect a carelessly written draft (at least we thought we could) if the handwriting was sloppy. But the word processor has changed all that. The draft that was written in 10 minutes may look pretty good. The student may even have had time to run it through spell check. Alas, what to do?

My advice is to begin with the assumption that you cannot be sure that you are reading a carelessly written paper. You may be looking at a paper by a student who has a learning disability, for example. Therefore, never make a comment such as, "You obviously spent very little time on this paper." You simply do not know. Instead, if, on the basis of reading a set of drafts, you think that a particular draft was just thrown together, discuss the main problems in the paper in your end comment and identify sentence level issues (just a few) on the first page. Try not to spend too much time on the paper. Invite the student to discuss other matters at the conference, or if a conference is not part of your program, then suggest an email or phone conversation about the paper.

Another problem: A student may submit the draft after the due date. For example, you are sound asleep. The clock says 2 am. You are awakened by a phone call from a distraught student who has suddenly realized that her instructor will not accept her paper without the attached draft and your comments. The paper is due 11 am the next morning. Can you read her draft in the student cafeteria over breakfast? My advice: Students need to recognize that deadlines are a fact of life. Apologize, but remain firm. Say you are very sorry, but the policy of the peer-tutoring program states that you read only the drafts that are submitted on time. However, as with all deadlines, there are always exceptions. If students have good reasons for submitting their drafts late, and you have the time, use your own judgment. However, beware of becoming a doormat for your fellow students. You will do more harm than good if you give students the impression that anything goes.

Conclusion

Whether you conference with students or comment in writing, or do both, you will find that most students appreciate your help. It seems fitting to end this chapter with a sampling of student reactions to our peer-tutoring program at La Salle:

- Mike was great to work with. His comments were very helpful and his criticism was never an issue. He was extremely helpful.
- Using the writing tutor helped me to make sure the paper I was handing in was clear and free of drastic errors.
- Having the writing tutor helped my grade and writing skills improve.
- He wrote just enough comments to describe and explain ways I could improve my paper and then we discussed them thoroughly in our meeting; he was extremely helpful!

Questions for Discussion and Writing

1. Read the assignment and the paper that could have been written in response to the assignment. You can use this paper to practice commenting in writing or at a conference.

The Assignment

Biology 156 Human Genetics
The first writing assignment is based upon the attached article, "Invisible Evidence." Select one of the cases in the article in which DNA fingerprinting was used. Discuss the advantages and disadvantages of using the technology in this case. You might want to include a discussion of the rights of the person involved, for example the right of the individual to privacy, the right to protect citizens from crime. Take a position for or against further

development and use of DNA fingerprinting in similar cases. Defend your argument logically with examples. Your audience is a fellow student with no familiarity about this issue. Therefore, you must provide background information and simplify your argument. Length: Approximately 3 pages.

Sample Student Paper

DNA FINGERPRINTING

In the past DNA, deoxyribonucleic Acid, was attributed to our eye color and inherited characteristics. Today DNA is playing an increasingly important role as evidence in United States Courts. A revolutionary process called DNA Fingerprinting is gaining widespread acceptance in our country's legal institutions. Although the process is still being researched, it enables us to extract the DNA from the smallest blood of hair or skin left at a crime scene and compare it with that of a suspect. Once this comparison is complete, if the two DNA prints match, the culprit is nabbed. Many hopeful molecular biologists are waiting for this technique to make the "fingerprint" obsolete.

This process of DNA Fingerprinting began to be recognized after the Federal Bureau of Investigations, the FBI, began to accumulate DNA records on database to aid in criminal cases. An estimated 1,000 court cases a year could benefit from this analysis of DNA. The innocent would be acquitted, while the guilty readily identified. Although this genetic analysis-is thought by some, to be a panacea for the rusty steel wheels of our present judicial system, there are others who are skeptical of the effectiveness and reliability of this newly pioneered field.

DNA Fingerprinting consists of several steps. First, small pieces of DNA are taken from a specimen. The DNA material is then divided and sorted according to size. Radioactive genetic probes are then applied to the sorted DNA material. These radioactive probes reveal gray and whitish bands on the DNA. DNA analysts study the highly variable regions of the chromosome with these gray bands. The most highly variable regions are studied and x-rayed to decrease the possibility of two people having the same reading. The regions analyzed reduce the likelihood of repetition to one in several billion.

This seemingly foolproof method does, however, have some drawbacks at present time. Firstly, since this process is so new, numerous institutions all have different methods of this process. A standardized process will have to be established for this to stand up in court. Secondly, scientists are undecided about the number of chromosomal regions that should be analyzed. One major problem with DNA Fingerprinting is the unknown frequency of certain chromosomal sections in the population as a whole and in its racial subsets.

There are also ethical questions to overcome with this analysis. Should the analysis include reporting of chromosomes responsible for abnormal behavior to testify as a character witness? Lastly, there is controversy pertaining to the constitutional rights of unwilling participants in this genetic analysis. This controversial area deals with the fourth amendment and due process of the law. To work through the specifics of these problems a meeting was held to fine tune the system. The members of this meeting will submit their findings to congress for review. Both scientists and law enforcement officials have high hopes for the future of fingerprinting. It is believed this process will not only apprehend the guilty but also aid in crime prevention. Some states have already begun saving DNA prints. These prints are expected to be immeasurably important for finding repeat sex offenders. it was thought hospitals would make use of such records by creating DNA files of newborns. This would be an active measure to prevent "babyswitching" and mix-ups in the nurseries.

Personally, I find this concept to be an important breakthrough in both science and in our judicial system. It would make our courts highly effective and also aid in other facets of social well being. DNA coding would help identify kidnap victims, as well as, apprehending the person who committed the crime. I believe our society is skeptical in general and many standards, rules, and a methodology; or genetic fingerprinting must be established in order to make it acceptable. This genetic coding is fascinating and revolutionary, once its flaws are corrected, genetic fingerprinting will be a means of concrete identification in our courts.

1a. Written Comments: If you choose to write comments, write a summary comment and comments in the margin. Swap your comments with another student in the class. Evaluate each other's comments using this checklist:
- Are the comments readerly and specific?
- Do they emphasize issues, which affect the whole paper?
- Are the comments clear?
- Does the end comment begin with "the positive?"
- Are the comments in the margin clear and specific?

1b. Model Conferences: If you choose the conference format to respond to this paper, one student should role-play the student who might have written this paper and one student should role-play the tutor. A third tutor can be the observer. The observer can take notes and answer such questions as, "What happened? What did the writer get out of the session? What was good about the session? (Gillespie, Lerner 62). If you are role playing the student, pretend that you are a freshman who is not biology major, but who is taking the course as a required course in a core curriculum. If you are role playing the tutor, or you are the observer, use this checklist to evaluate a 20-minute conference:

- Are the tutor and the student sitting side by side?
- Is there a pad available for taking notes?
- Has the tutor made an effort to "get acquainted?"
- Does the tutor ask open-ended questions to learn about the writing assignment and the student's attitudes about writing or the assignment?
- Does the tutor focus on the major problem in the paper?
- Does the tutor give the student the opportunity to talk?
- Does the tutor encourage the student to do the writing?
- Does the tutor end the conference by summing up?

2. Review your instructor's comments on a paper you have written recently. Analyze these comments using the checklist in Exercise 1a for critiquing written comments. How would you rate your instructor's comments?

3. Write a 2–3 page paper on the topic, "The Benefits of Peer Tutoring in Writing." Pretend that your audience consists of freshmen. Your goal is to encourage them to use the writing center. Swap your paper with another peer tutor. One of you should play the tutor. Conference for 20 minutes. If you play the student, discuss your plan for revising the paper as a result of the conference. Also, discuss your feelings as a "tutee." If you role-play the tutor, review the conference using the checklist in Exercise 1b.

Works Cited

Carino, Peter. "Power and Authority in Peer Tutoring. The Center Will Hold." *Critical Perspectives on the Writing Center*. Logan, UT: Utah State University Press, 2003.

Flynn, Thomas and Mary King. *The Dynamics of the Writing Conference: Social and Cognitive Interaction*. Urbana, IL: NCTE, 1993.

Gillespie, Paula and Neal Lerner. *The Allyn and Bacon Guide to Peer Tutoring*. Needham Heights, MA: Pearson Education Co., 2000.

Harris, Muriel. *Teaching One to One: The Writing Conference*. Urbana, IL: NCTE, 1986.

Raforth, Ben, Ed. *A Tutor's Guide: Helping Writers One to One*.
    Portsmouth, NH: Boynton/Cook Publishers, 2000.
Reigstad, Thomas and Donald A. McAndrew. *Training Tutors for Writing
    Conferences*. Urbana, IL: NCTE, 1984.
Soven, Margot. *Teaching Writing in Middle and Secondary Schools*.
    Needham Heights, MA: Allyn and Bacon, 1999.
Straub, Richard, Ed. *A Sourcebook for Responding to Student Writing*.
    Cresskill, NJ: Hampton Press, 1999.

For Further Reading

Branscomb, Eric. "Types of Conferences and the Composing Process."
    The Writing Center Journal 7 (1986): 27–35.
Maxwell, Martha. *When Tutor Meets Student*. 2nd ed. Ann Arbor, MI:
    University of Michigan Press, 2000.
Morrow, Diane Seltzer. "Tutoring Writing: Healing or What?" *College
    Composition and Communication* 42 (1991): 218–229.
Walvoord, Barbara. *Helping Students Write Well*. 2nd ed. New York:
    MLA, 1986.

4

Common Writing Problems: Focus, Organization, Development, Style, and Correctness

This chapter will focus on specific writing problems, how to identify them, and how to help students solve them, but, as in previous chapters, the students will be our main focus. Every student's goal is to write a good paper, and the role of the tutor is to identify the characteristics of his writing which prevent him from achieving that aim. To help the student accomplish his objective, we must read the paper keeping in mind the general conventions of academic writing which most instructors expect in written work. We'll use the term *problems*, despite its negative connotation, to identify characteristics of papers which don't conform to the general conventions of academic writing.

Critiquing papers, like learning any skill, requires experience and perhaps trial and error as well. Don't expect to be able to identify immediately, and then solve, all the common problems in a paper—though you will get better at it with practice. Tori Haring-Smith, formerly at Brown University, has said that in her experience most writing tutors reach their stride in their third semester as tutors. I would say that it is during the second semester that I notice tutors becoming more confident about their ability to recognize the kinds of problems that prevent students from getting good grades and acquiring the tutoring skills that help students both recognize and solve these problems.

For example, after his second semester as a writing tutor, Ryan Hoffmaster wrote,

> Dr. Soven,
>
> I think this semester's experience was unique in that I was able to gain a sense of my independence as a writing tutor. I got much better at helping students improve their papers by recognizing obvious problems in them. In doing so, I believe I have developed confidence and even a bit of expertise in my role as a peer tutor.

Once Ryan was able to identify issues which would help the student improve the paper at hand, he was able to focus on some of the long-range goals of peer tutoring.

Where to Start? The Students' Goals

Let's pretend that a student walks into the writing center with a first draft. Let's also pretend that the assignment instructions are fairly clear. When you first see this draft—either in the writing center or as a Writing Fellow, think about what matters most to the majority of students. Most students want a good grade on the essay. Period, the end. The smart move now is to encourage positive attitudes towards peer tutoring by meeting the student's short-range goals first. In the process, you can begin to model and encourage the kinds of social and cognitive behaviors that lead to accomplishing the long-range objectives of teaching composition related to the expressivist, cognitive, and social constructionist theories discussed in Chapter 1.

If you buy into the idea that it is part of your job to motivate students to accomplish these long-range goals—becoming full-fledged members of the academic community (social constructionist theory), helping them develop effective strategies for negotiating each stage of the writing process (coginitivist theory), and using the assignment to express their own ideas (expressivism)—you must gain the trust of your tutees. Just as you cannot become an expert tutor during your first tutoring session, students cannot achieve the long-range goals associated with learning how to write in their first encounter with a peer tutor. Research tells us that in most cases students don't arrive at a comfort zone in the academic community that allows them to speak and write with confidence until they are seniors! Adopting a process approach to writing, learning the importance of drafting and revising is a prerequisite for membership.

Students' Short-Range Goals

Question: Does the draft meet the all of the objectives of the assignment?

This is a simple question, but surprisingly the most frequent problem that writing tutors at La Salle encounter, both in the writing center and in the Writing Fellows program, is the *distance* between the draft and the assignment instructions. The instructor may believe that he or she has been eminently clear and the student may believe that he or she has followed the assignment instructions. So what goes wrong? Well, some research indicates that students transform assignments to tasks they can accomplish, especially when the assignment is too difficult for them. We turn once again to the research on cognition to understand how novice writers approach writing assignments (Flower 5). For example, a common assignment is the book review, which requires a summary and a critique. Students often can handle the summary part of the assignment, but are not sure how to evaluate the book, so they ignore that part of the assignment.

Another reason that students may ignore the critique part of the assignment is related to social constructionist theory. As David Bartholomae points out in his landmark essay, "Inventing the University," students are asked to behave like academics before they have the knowledge or confidence to assume that role. Bartholomae says that students must sound like academics while they are "still confused about what academic discourse calls for" (Flower 4). The book review is frequently assigned in introductory course when students are not yet ready to assume a critical stance.

Once you realize that the student has omitted part of the assignment, then begins the process of rereading and interpreting the assignment together. The student can contribute to this discussion by summarizing the teacher's explanation of the assignment in class, if the teacher did indeed elaborate on the assignment instructions. If not, then you may need to draw on your own experience with similar assignments. If you are not sure, find out what composition texts say about the assignment in question (for example Behrens and Rosen) or consult a text such as *Write to Learn: A Guide to Writing Across the Curriculum* (Soven) which includes a comprehensive description of assignments typically assigned in college.

However, keep in mind Bartholomae's point that students must follow the guidelines for academic writing before they fully understand their purpose. They have one foot in the community before they feel like full-fledged members. That advice may sound contradictory, but when I think about how I learned to drive, it makes sense. My father kept saying "90% of driving is watching the other guy." I kept gazing at the rear view and side view mirrors during my driving lessons. I didn't really understand the significance of that statement, though, until I my first "fender bender." Then I felt like I was a real driver. The accident was in a sense a form of initiation which made me behave like a driver.

Question: Does the paper have a thesis?

Most essays require an overall focus that addresses the assignment question. I say, *most*, because some assignments do not require a thesis statement. Writing tutors often make the mistake of searching for a thesis when in fact the assignment doesn't call for one. For example, the autobiography often assigned in education courses or nursing courses comes to mind. These assignments require a chronological narrative of life experiences without a thesis statement at the beginning of the paper.

Drafts with *thesis* problems come in several varieties: for example, the paper with no discernible thesis. In my experience these are quite rare. More typical is the paper with a thesis that is too general or that is buried deep in the body of the paper, forcing the reader to wander through the paper searching for the thesis: For example, for the assignment, "Compare and contrast the treatment of an environmental issue in Biology 154 to the treatment of an environmental issue from the perspective of another discipline. Be sure to demonstrate how each course approached similar aspects of the issue," a hypothetical paper from student X might take this form.

> On the surface, the courses in which I am presently enrolled seem quite different. Looking beyond the exterior, similarities are discovered. Many areas in History may be connected to ecological subjects. Urbanization is taught in both courses.
>
> In History 151, Global History, taught by [teacher A], the topic of was dealt with when Europe's industrial revolution was discussed. Historically, the industrial revolution lead to an unprecedented urbanization of world society. The size of cities traditionally had depended on the amount of food that the surrounding land could produce. Thus the most populous cities were in the valleys and flood plains. It also stated in Introduction to Environmental Studies second edition, the text for Biology 154, that "the first cities arose along the Tigris and Euphrates rivers roughly 6000 years ago."

Due to the Industrial Revolution and the factory system, a mass influx flooded the new centers of industry. The point was elaborated in Bio 154. People moved into the cities to be closer to their employment. This is how cities expand.

Technological and medical advances eliminated plagues (external over the population) which had previously decimated cities. Advances in centralized sewerage waste disposal and the insurance of clean water and an adequate food supply brought the rapid growth of cities.

Included with the similarities in my Ecology and History course there is one difference. My History course tends to deal with urbanization of the 16th century. Whereas in my Ecology urbanization is given more emphasis. Although the concepts concern different time periods the ideas are similar.

Similar views on urbanization were presented in both History 151 and Bio 150.

Student X most likely thinks that he or she has a thesis related to the assignment. But, given the assignment question, the thesis should not only name the topic, which seems to be *urbanization,* but tell the reader something about the differences between how the topic of urbanization is treated from a historical versus a biological perspective.

The rest of the paper is a bit of a hodgepodge, but the student seems to be saying that both in the biology course and the history course he or she learned that cities develop where the people can grow crops; they expand as they experience the industrial revolution, and survive due to advances in sanitation that eliminate plagues.

Any draft that does not have a clear thesis needs major surgery. Luckily they won't all be as bad as my example. An easy way to get started is to suggest that the student use the tried and true *essay question* writing technique.

- Suggest that the student underline the key words in the assignment: (for example in the assignment in p. 77 key words are *compare, contrast, environmental issue,* and so on).
- Talk about how the introductory paragraph needs to say something about all of these topics.
- If you are working on the paper at a conference, now is the time to have a general conversation in which you help the student clarify his ideas about the topic.
- Be sure that student has rewritten the introduction or at least has some notes when the conference ends.

Question: If the draft has a thesis what is the quality of the argument itself?

You may be so relieved to read a draft which seems to have both met the assignment requirements and has a thesis that you look no further, and now here is where I violate my advice to ignore thinking about grades. The fact is that a paper will most likely not receive an "A" grade if it simply scratches the surface of the topic. Although you are not thinking about grades, it is your responsibility to give suggestions to the student whose paper is good, but could be better. There is always room for improvement. For example, in my *Scoring Guide for Academic Essays*, I suggest that a *superior* response has these qualities:

- The essay shows substantial depth, fullness, and complexity of thought.
- The essay demonstrates clear, focused, unified, and coherent organization and is fully developed and detailed.
- The essay evidences superior control of word choice, sentence variety, and is free from major errors. (Adapted from White, 1995)

Here is an example of a paper that has a weak thesis, but eventually seems to answer the assignment question. But does the response show "substantial depth, fullness, and complexity of thought"? Below is the assignment from one of my freshman composition courses:

Describe a tradition with which you are acquainted, whether a national, ethnic, family, or personal one. As part of your description, you should discuss what significance this tradition supposedly has. A good paper would also consider whether the tradition retains any significance, or has become merely a hollow ritual, and why. (You may of course include your own reasons for accepting or rejecting the tradition [. . .]) Focus your attention on only one tradition for this paper.

And a student essay that might have been written in response to this assignment:

I come from a Polish-Mexican background. In my family there are many traditions because of the great differences between the two cultures. I will focus on one special Polish tradition and that is the breaking of Oplatki.

The breaking Oplatki is always done on Christmas eve before the main meal of the evening. There is usually a large crowd because all of the relatives from my mother's side gather together this night to celebrate Christmas.

Oplatki is a thin wafer like edible food shaped in a rectangle and sometimes stamped with a Nativity scene or other Christmas scene. It is white, usually but can be tinted pink. Each person receives a sizable portion of Oplatki. After prayers are said the breaking begins. Each person there goes to every relative and breaks his piece of Oplatki. In turn, that relative breaks the piece off the other person's. It is then eaten. After this, the two people show some sign of affection toward each other by a kiss or a hug. This goes on till everyone has given a piece of Oplatki to everyone else.

This tradition is also Catholic. Its significance is that we should all be brothers especially united since we are in the same family. It is done on Christmas because Christ's birth symbolized the beginning or starting over again. The best way to start a new year is to get rid of old grudges, settle differences, and be on good terms with one another. The bread is symbolic Holy Communion. We all participate are therefore united in some way.

After taking part and observing this tradition this past Christmas, I realized that it is still very significant and important to almost everyone. There are seldom arguments or long term grudges in our family and this tradition may have something to do with this fact. The younger children in our family also participate in this and I think it is good for them to be raised on this tradition.

My own reasons for accepting this is partly because I was raised in the tradition by mainly because I can see the good that it does and can appreciate my relatives as friends.

The writer says that the significance of the Oplatki ritual is that "we should all be brothers" and "that when one shares the Oplatki, all grudges are left behind and differences are settled." She concludes that this ritual may be the reason that her family is free of these problems. However, as a reader I would like to know if there are other possible reasons for the harmony in this family. I might respond, "Maybe the Oplatki ritual simply validates a quality that your family has nurtured in other ways." The writer can strengthen the paper by writing about that possibility.

Another reason that papers sound "thin" is related to the insufficient development of the ideas in the papers. When papers lack sufficient examples, or the examples themselves lack detail, essays seem to lack ideas. Short paragraphs are often a tell-tale sign of insufficient development. Notice the paragraphs in the Oplatki paper and the Biology/History comparison paper.

One tutor's comment about a paper written in a philosophy class illustrates one way to address weak development: "My favorite part of your paper is your example of a moral dilemma—should the man return the excess change to the store? In fact, I think if you could come up with some other examples at other points in your paper, you could make it stronger" (Victoria Franz). Victoria sounds like a reader genuinely interested in more information.

Question: Is the draft organized effectively at the macrolevel?
These are the three questions we ask about "organization":

1. Is the organization logical given the nature of the topic? For example, if I am writing about "my day" it would be logical to begin with breakfast.
2. Is the organization effective? If I am writing about "my day" I might choose to begin with the most astonishing part of the day rather than adopt a chronological approach to organizing the material. Countless times I have written on students' papers "I'm not sure why you chose to write about Topic 1 in the essay before you wrote about Topic 2. Can you explain?" I think that some students are so relieved to have covered all parts of the assignment that they often do not have any cognitive energy or patience to think about the alternative organizational possibilities.
3. Is the paper disjointed? For example, does the student who is writing about his day describe breakfast at several points in the paper? Most disjointed papers have organization problems that are more difficult to identify than they are in an essay in which the contents can be organized chronologically. Many subjects require an organizational plan based on the logic inherent in the subject. The "Comparison of the Biology and History Courses" paper is a good example of a paper with disjointed organization.

How do we tackle a paper with problems in organization. Don't start from scratch by suggesting a new outline, unless you want to confront a crestfallen student. Make readerly comments in the margin, such as "I find it hard to follow your line of thinking here. How does this part fit in? What's the point of this section? How does this paragraph relate to what you just said? Your introduction made me expect to hear about X next, but this is about Y." In the conference situation you can suggest that the student makes a list of main point of each paragraph and review that list for the issues just discussed. Is the organization logical? Is the organization effective? Is the organization disjointed? A new outline can be generated as a result of evaluating the organization of the paper in this way.

Kenneth Bruffee recommends using a descriptive outline instead of a "main point" outline to determine if the organization of the paper is helping to accomplish its aim. The student annotates the paper by describing the function of each paragraph in relation to the essay's proposition. This exercise can also help the student evaluate the techniques he or she has used to develop the ideas in the essay. Here[1] are some of the many functions a paragraph can perform:

Tells a story	Analyzes
Gives reasons	Synthesizes
Describes	Defines a term
Explains	Gives examples
Compares	

Question: Does the paper have stylistic problems?
Some students use the term *style* as a descriptive term for the entire paper. They say "My teachers don't like my style." When they learn that the word refers to sentence level issues, they are quite surprised. Other students confuse the term *style* with the term *grammar*. When you recommend avoiding using *this* as a pronoun, these students will respond, "I've always been bad at grammar." Before you begin talking about style, be sure that you clear up confusion about the meaning of the term. Style involves the choice of words you use to talk about a subject. Words like *formal, informal, colloquial,* and *academic* apply to style. Phrases such as *too wordy* also apply to style. Explain that what distinguishes stylistic concerns from grammar errors is that grammar errors are violations of the structural conventions of standard English. Relatively stable rules of correctness govern pronoun cases, subject-verb agreement, dangling modifiers, parallelism, and sentence completeness. In contrast, stylistic concerns involve choices. For example, we choose a more formal style for academic papers than we use in conversation or a letter to a friend.

Most assignments require an academic style. Here are just a few examples of the kinds of words and expressions which signal a departure from the academic style:

- Contractions
- Colloquial language such as *first of all.*

---

[1]Adapted from Bruffee, 1993 (166).

- Overuse of the word *thing* and the word *this* as pronouns (for example, "By this women are going to be exactly equal to their male rivals.") Being specific is an important characteristic of an academic style.
- The expressions *I think* or *I feel.*

When it comes to style, it's often hard to make a logical case for avoiding certain words and expressions. Remember Bruffee's description of the tutor as translator. For example, it's your responsibility to explain to your tutees that the first person pronoun is not typically used in academic essays. Instructors don't want you to say, "I feel that." The use of *I feel* makes your argument sound weak. Academics believe that arguments are based on evidence, not feelings. You can explain that academics admire precision and specificity, but do not be surprised if your tutees do not look convinced. They will probably think that these *rules* sound arbitrary until they recognize the rationale for specificity and accuracy.

Question: Is the draft free of errors in grammar, punctuation, and spelling? If not, how do you respond?

Here are some very common errors:

Error in agreement between subject and verb
Incorrect: The advantages for *women* as equals, except in the case of equal pay for equal work *is* very few.
Correct: The advantages for women as equals, except in the case of equal pay for equal work are very few.

Error in agreement between subject and pronoun
Incorrect: When the *reader* reads this particular passage, *they* may feel that [...]
Correct: When the *reader* reads this particular passage, *he* or *she* may feel that [...]

Often students will catch errors in agreement if you ask them to read the offending sentence aloud. We rarely make errors in agreement when speaking.

Punctuation errors
Students view punctuation as a mine field. Probably as early as seventh grade most students learn the correct use of the comma, the semi-colon, the colon, and so on, but even Writing Tutors tell me that they use the *inspirational* approach to punctuation. However, take heart. Some errors

are more typical and more identifiable than others. For example, students often get confused between compound sentences, which require commas, and compound phrases, which do not require commas.

Compound sentences
The rule: Use a comma between a conjunction (and, but, for, or, nor, so, yet) linking two independent clauses.
Incorrect: He is a terrific athlete and he is also a great student.
Correct: He is a terrific athlete, and he is also a great student.

Compound phrases
The rule: Compound phrases join words, or phrases, to show addition, contrast, or choice. There is no comma required before the conjunction.
Incorrect: He is a terrific athlete, and also a great student.
Correct: He is a terrific athlete and also a great student.

Punctuation errors, unlike errors in agreement, may not be solved by asking the student to read the problematic sentence aloud. Pauses are not necessarily to be trusted as signals for punctuation. Give the student the bad news. There is no way around learning the rules of punctuation. However, you should try to avoid using grammatical terminology when discussing these rules. For example, there is no point in saying "you never put a comma before a conjunctive adverb like *however*, but you can say that *however* is not equivalent to *and* or *but*". "It takes a capitol letter when it connects two ideas." Needless to say, there is much more to say about sentence level errors. My suggestion: review the rules of punctuation and study the "common error" list which most handbooks include or you can find online.

Problem: Errors that are difficult to classify
Many sentence errors do not fit into *neat categories* such as comma and agreement errors. Valerie Krishna's article *The Syntax of Error* is one of the most illuminating discussions of these kinds of hard-to-classify errors.

The examples she gives are typical of many student papers:

1. In regard to the Watergate affair and the recent problems that the White House is involved with, it is of concern to all citizens.
2. The use of the pilgrimage was to create to make the scene more realistic.
3. His concern for outward appearances is mainly to use it to convey the inner character.

4. Man has invented various types of poisons to kill insects: among the surviving insects, they have all become immune to poisons.
5. Limiting the open enrollment program won't help solve the problem.

Sentences like these are often the result of what handbooks call *shifts*, "an unnecessary or illogical change in tense, voice, mood, person, number, tone [...]" (Random House) or a mixed construction. However, as Krishna points out, unlike comma errors or agreement errors, no one can anticipate all the different ways a piece of writing might be illogical or incoherent. She suggests trying to "understanding the approach that leads to these kinds of sentences" (187). Krishna believes that students who write this way "habitually back into their sentences, putting the heart of their idea into prepositional phrases, object noun clauses, adjectives, adverbs, or other ancillary parts of the sentences, wasting the subject and/or verb position on indefinite evasive expressions such as 'it is,' 'it appears,' 'this seems to be the case [...]' " (188).

Krishna's method for tackling these kinds of sentences seems to work. First, ask the student to identify the central ideal of the sentence:

> Generally if one asks the writer of the Watergate sentence what is the subject of the sentence, he will answer "Watergate affair," "recent problems" (or both) or "White House"; that is he will name the logical subject of the sentence. The teacher [in our case, the peer tutor] can explain to the student that the logical subject and the grammatical subject ought to coincide and instruct the student to recompose the sentence using the logical subject as the grammatical subject. (188)

For example, "The Watergate affair and the recent problems that the White House is involved with are of concern to all citizens" (189). This is not a terrific sentence, but it is better than the student's first effort.

Krishna's approach sounds time consuming, and it is. And possibly only the highly motivated student will catch on. However, understanding the problem and the possible solution for sentences which defy typical categories of error should help you to feel more confident as you read student papers.

Conclusion

This chapter focused on the *general student*, although we know that's a bit of a fiction. Perhaps it's more accurate to say that we focused on an important objective for most students—that is to get a good grade, and how we can help them identify problems in their papers which stand in their way. The next chapter will focus on tailoring tutoring strategies for the variety of students you will tutor.

Questions for Discussion and Writing

1. Read Jaime Longo's description of her style of writing as a freshman. Choose a paper which you wrote either during your high school or college courses. Describe its strengths and weaknesses. Use the questions in the chapter as a guide (one page). Be sure to comment on your *style* of writing. How does your style of writing as a freshman compare to Jaime's style of writing?

   > I chose a paper that I wrote at the end of my freshman year of high school because I find the stylistic errors to be quite amusing from my current perspective. It would seem that at that time I was struggling with the language of academic discourse. My first paragraph, which is actually a really long sentence, is full of "thesaurus" words, as is the rest of the paper. The words themselves are not incorrect or inapplicable, but when combined, they make very pretentious sentences. The diction throughout the paper is very sophisticated for a fourteen year old, but I can tell that there are times when I could tell that my younger self did not know exactly what the words meant, only that the essay sounded professional. Other times I substituted phrases where the one word would have been fine. My favorite substitution is "parental fatigue" for "parental."
   >
   > My pretentious diction, combined with a few other problems such as grammatical errors and stylistic glitches seem characteristic of my style. I also used capitalized words for emphasis, like NEVER MUST. There are also occasional shifts in narrative voice such as "You need to know [...]" and then later on "One must [...]"
   >
   > I keep this paper on hand to remind myself how far I've come.
   >
   > For all of its faults, it's not a bad paper for a freshman in high school. But looking at this paper reinforces the idea that writing is not static; it is forever evolving, and if seven years from now, I look back at my college papers, I will probably be surprised again at my progress!

2. Discuss the strengths and weaknesses of the two following papers as comprehensively as possible. Use the questions in the chapter as a guide.

The Assignment

(I have used this assignment in introductory literature courses.)

Read "A Wife's Story" by Bharati Mukherjee.

Write an essay (3–4 pages) on the following topic:

Discuss Panna's attitude towards American society. What does she like about the people she has met? What does she dislike? Why does she decide that the benefits of life in America outweigh the drawbacks of living in America.

Sample Student Paper

"A Wife's Story"

In the short story, "A Wife's Story", Panna is an Indian woman living in America. She struggles at times to embrace culture, but seems to love America anyway. Her experiences with the things she loves seem to overbear the things she does not.

The story opens with her and her former country being ridiculed much to the pleasure of an audience in a theatre. She does not quite understand why nobody seems to care that her self-worth is being trampled on. Even her friend with her at the theatre is chuckling about the insults.

Next, she leaves the theatre trying to remember how her American friends told her that insults were a part of an acceptance. She leaves the theatre with her friend, Imre, who is of Russian descent, and he calms her down. He hugs her and holds her, very unlike her brothers or husband. This is the first sense of her being delighted about America.

Panna thinks back to the way her culture is back in India. She knows her brothers nor her husband would have held her close in the middle of a street. Panna enjoys this type of embracement here in America. Her friend Imre, who has a wife and two kids, was merely holding her just to be a courteous gentleman. His uprising taught him to act that way around a woman who is scared.

Following her cab ride with Imre, Panna goes to her residence. She walks in and has a discussion with Charity, her oriental roommate. She enjoys how her roommate though flat-chested, can be a model here in America. She also seems to enjoy Charity's family, mainly her humpbacked uncle. Charity's uncle reminds her of family, and his presence seems to present a sense of comfort to Panna.

The next section of the story has a few references to things and people she does not like in America. When she goes to meet her husband at the airport, she makes sure she puts on her jewelry. She mentions that she doesn't always wear jewelry because "who knows when, or whom, desire will overwhelm." Following this was reference about not wearing a gold ring. She said that Americans know Indian woman have 24-kt jewelry so it makes them a target.

After spending a few days with her husband Panna goes on a tour with him around New York City, the setting of the story. She notices how professional the tour guide looks and even describes him. Saying he looks like an actor with blow-dried hair. She then proceeded to not even like the tour, but still thought the tour guide was professional.

During the same tour a European takes a picture of Panna and her husband with their camera since they had trouble working it. He then flirts with Panna and offers them a drink. Panna enjoys the comfort and after seeing how her day went decides that it would be best if she went back to India with him. Her thinks all men are watching her, and he does not pleasure he gives her, but her husband seems to think he is a creep. Her husband want her to fall in love with one of them. He sees them as cheats, but she sees these courteous flirting men in a different light.

Panna likes the people she meets in America because they offer comfort. Each one she liked in the story seemed to present to her some type of comfort. Comfort, as the story progressed, was shown as a very important feature in Panna's life. She became comfortable around her husband, and waits for him to make love to her. She has seemed to gain self-esteem throughout the story despite being insulted in the beginning. Despite having her heritage insulted in America, she found that other people offered more comfort than others in her homeland. She enjoyed this extra sense of comfort and that appeared to outweigh the people she did not like throughout the story.

Assignment: Introductory course in religion taught by Br. Charles Echelmeier

Below are several observations about the nature of the narrative style (the *How* of story telling) in the Hebrew Scriptures. The stories are brief and characterization emerges from what the characters say and do rather than from description.

There are few abstract nouns. Sentences tend to be short and simple. The appeal of the narrative is emotional rather than intellectual. There is internal evidence of an earlier oral tradition behind the text.

Pick out several of these characteristics and write an essay in which you describe *How* the story (stories) contained in the first 23 chapters of the Book of Exodus is told.

All papers should be in an acceptable style. Spelling and grammar should be at least minimally at college level. I will be particularly severe in my reaction to names, words, and so on that appear in the text that there should be no reason for you to spell incorrectly: *Israel*, for example. Length: Maximum 3 pages.

Sample Student Paper

How The Hebrew Scriptures Are Told

The stories of the Hebrew scriptures have some special characteristics. The stories are brief, characteristics emerge from actions rather than descriptions, and the sentence structure is short and brief. When the elements are put together one gets a feel for how the Hebrew scriptures are told

The sentence structure of the Hebrew scriptures is short and brief. There are no complex sentences in the Hebrew scriptures. An example of this short and brief sentence structure can be found in Exodus 8:3. "But the magicians did the same by their magic arts." That sentence was taken right after Aaron used the staff to overrun Egypt with frogs. There is an effect that this short and brief sentence structure gives the reader. Without long, complicated sentences the reader is drawn right into what is being written. This also allows for a little bit of interpretation on the reader's Dart. The event is not described in detail. It's left up to the reader to formulate their own image of what is going on.

These short sentences in turn lead to short stories. Most of the stories in Exodus range anywhere from a quarter to a half of a page. This also has an important function. It keeps the reader reading. Longer stories tend to drag on, and some of what is being said is lost along the way. The writer makes his point about the story quick and then gets out.

Because the stories are short there is no room for descriptive passages on how a particular character feels. Instead, the characters' traits are literally shown to us by what they say and do. We can tell that Moses is a very brave man. It does not say anywhere in the text that he is brave, but you can tell by his actions. He confronts Pharaoh, who at this time is a very powerful individual. Pharaoh has all of the Israelites enslaved, and what does Moses do? He approaches Pharaoh and says, "Let my people go." This takes an awful lot of courage, but no where does it say specifically that Moses is brave. Pharaoh, on the other hand, is seen to be an individual who is not very bright. He tells Moses after the fourth plague, "I will let you go to offer sacrifice to the Lord, your God, in the desert, provided that you do not go far away and that you pray for me." This tells us two things about Pharaoh. First, he is not the smartest person in the world. Pharaoh is willing to let the slaves go away from him to pray. Only a person of very low intelligence would allow his slaves to do something like that, because they may escape. It also tells us that Pharaoh does not put that much faith in his God. This gives you the idea that the God of Moses was more powerful.

With all of these characteristics put together you can start to see how the Hebrew scriptures are told. Through the use of short sentences and stories, as well as characterizing people by what they say and do, you get a very straight forward story. This also leaves itself open to the imagination as well With the lack of some details the reader can then have many images in their mind.

Works Cited

Behrens, Laurence and Leonard Rosen. *Write to Learn: A Guide to Writing Across the Curriculum*. 8th ed. New York: Longman, 2002.

Bruffee, Kenneth. *A Short Course in Writing*. 4th ed. New York: Harper Collins, 1993.

Diederich, Paul. "In Praise of Praise." *A Guide for Evaluating Composition*. Ed. Sister H. Judine, IHM. Urbana, IL: NCTE, 1965.

Flower, Linda. *Negotiating Academic Discourse. Read to Write Report #10. Center for the Study of Writing*, University of California, Berkeley, Carnegie Mellon University, Pittsburgh, PA: May, 1989.

Flower, Linda and John R. Hayes, "The Cognition of Discovery: Defining a Rhetorical Problem." *The Writing Teacher's Sourcebook*. 2nd ed. Ed. Gary Tate and Edward P. J. Corbett. New York: Oxford University Press, 1988.

Grimm, Nancy Maloney. "Rearticulating the Work of the Writing Center." *College Composition and Communication* 47:4 (1996): 523–548.

Haring-Smith, Tori. "Changing Students' Attitudes: Writing Fellows Programs." *Writing Across the Curriculum: A Guide to Developing Programs*. Eds. Susan H. McLeod and Margot Soven. SAGE: Newbury, CA, 1992.

Ryan, Leigh. *The Bedford Guide to Writing Tutors*. 2nd ed. Boston, MA: Bedford Books, 1998.

Kail, Harvey and John Trimbur. "The Politics of Peer Tutoring." *WPA: Writing Program Administration* 11:1–2 (1987): 511–512.

Soven, Margot. *Write to Learn: A Guide to Writing Across the Curriculum*. Cincinnatti, OH: South-Western Publishing, 1996.

———. *Teaching Writing in Middle and Secondary Schools*. Boston, MA: Allyn and Bacon, 1999.

Walvoord, Barbara E. Fassler. *Helping Students Write Well*. 2nd ed. New York: MLA, 1986.

White, Edward. *Assigning, Responding, and Evaluating: A Teachers Guide*. 2nd ed. New York: St. Martins Press, 1992.

For Further Reading

Connors, Robert J. and Andrea Lunsford. "Frequency of Formal Errors in Current College Writing, or Ma and Pa Kettle Do Research." *College Composition and Communication* 39 (1988): 395–409.

Harris, Joseph. "Error." *Teaching Composition: Background Readings*. Ed. T. R. Johnson and Shirley Morahan. Boston, MA: Bedford/St. Martins, 2002.

Schwartz, Mimi. "Revision Profiles: Patterns and Implications." *College English* 45 (1983): 549–558.

Shaughnessy, Mina. *Errors and Expectations*. New York: Oxford University Press, 1977.

Straub, Richard. *The Practice of Response: Strategies for Commenting on Student Writing*. Cresskill, NJ: Hampton Press, 2000.

Trimbur, John R. *Writing with Style: Conversations on the Art of Writing*. 2nd ed. Saddle River, NJ: Prentice-Hall, 2000.

CHAPTER

5

The Writing Process of College Students

In all honesty, my first real learning experience with writing occurred in college. I really felt as if I was learning for the first time. My grades at the undergraduate level were virtually the same as my grades in high school. I never considered planning, drafting, and revising when I was writing my papers. When I think about how I wrote papers, the first draft was the final draft.

—Eric Kellich, Writing Tutor

In high school Eric, a former writing tutor at La Salle, was not asked to write drafts of his papers. In Eric's English courses most of the time was devoted to learning literature, not to writing. This book is not the right place to examine the reasons for the lack of writing instruction in high school, but we do know things are getting better. The National Writing Project, a federally funded project to improve the teaching of writing, for example, has had considerable impact on writing instruction in high schools. However, I still meet students who attended high schools where they were not taught strategies for planning, drafting, and editing their papers, and there were few opportunities for peer review.

In contrast, in colleges and universities, a process approach to teaching composition was implemented more rapidly on a national scale. You can be fairly sure that most of the students you meet in the writing center have taken a course in freshman composition in which the writing process was stressed. Most likely, these students were introduced to all stages of the writing process: free writing, planning, drafting, revising, and editing. Instead of starting from scratch, when you talk about drafting and revising you can probably assume that they have been introduced to the composing process in their freshman composition course or its equivalent—perhaps a freshman seminar in which writing is stressed. However, for a variety of reasons, most students do not actually write their papers this way (surprise, surprise!). Why do students have trouble meeting the length requirement of assignments? Why do many students start their papers the night (or morning) before the deadline? Why don't they even bother using spell check?

Chapters 1–4 were designed to give you the survival skills you need to start tutoring and an overview of theory and research which support the strategies discussed in the first half of the book. For you to hone these skills, to apply them selectively, you need to know more about the main parts of the tutoring equation: the students, the assignments, and the tutoring process itself.

Theory and Research

The more you know about the writing process of your tutees, the better your chances of helping them develop more effective strategies for writing their papers: what goes on in their minds as they first begin a writing assignment then, after they have a draft, how do they feel about revising, and so on.

What did Hayes and Flower mean when they said that "the novice writer is on cognitive overload, like a 'switchboard operator' who must juggle demands on her attention and constraints on what she can do" ("Writer-Based Prose" 30). All writers experience trouble when the task becomes too hard, but novice writers often experience problems even when the task is within their reach because they do not tackle writing tasks in stages. They try to do everything at once. Although it is the case that these stages often overlap, the experienced writer is aware of the pitfalls of shortchanging any of them.

Allan Glatthorn has developed a model of the composing process describing the mental activity and behaviors that accompany each stage of the composing process of experienced writers. His model is quite useful for thinking about the methods used by novice writers in contrast to experienced writers.

A Model of the Composing Process: Experienced Writers

Stage	Mental Activity	Behavior

1. Exploring	Considering subjects
	Thinking of an angle
	Reviewing memory
	Identifying information
	  needed
	Considering voice, tone
	Thinking about audience
	Weighing points
	Thinking about medium
		Jotting Notes
		Asking questions
		Trying out ideas
		Retrieving
		  information

2. Planning	Choosing points
	Deciding about order
	Deciding about
	  general form
	Choosing beginning
	  strategy
	Deciding on voice, tone
		Making notes
		Making diagrams
		Making sketches
		Talking about
		  choices
		Making outlines

3. Drafting	Trying out places
	  of sentences
	Searching for words
	Thinking about
	  paragraph shape
		Mumbling, testing
		  words
		Writing phrases,
		  sentences

4. Revising and
  Editing
	Reading what
	  has been written
	Trying out other words
	Trying out other
	  sentence patterns
	Looking for errors
	Re-thinking choices
		Crossing out
		Adding parts
		Re-arranging parts
		Correcting errors
		Changing words

5. Sharing	Deciding what is
	  to be shared
	Deciding on medium
	  of sharing
		Reading aloud
		Posting
		Publishing

Exploring and Planning

Flower and Hayes documented the methods used by experienced writers to work through each of these stages, from the moment they receive a writing task, or present one to themselves, to the time it is completed. For example, experienced writers spend considerable effort during the planning stage, developing an image of the purpose and audience for their writing. Flower and Hayes state, "They build a unique representation, not only of their audience and assignment, but also of their goals involving the audience, their own persona [as writers] and the text. By contrast novice writers think primarily about form, such as the number of pages required" (Tate/Corbett 99). Furthermore, good writers "create a particularly rich set of goals for affecting their reader which helps them to generate new ideas" (Tate/Corbett 100). Experienced writers also continue to develop new goals as they continue to write. But, in contrast, novice writers stay with the initial, perhaps limited, view of the writing task, which restricts their ability to generate ideas as the writing develops. Experienced writers also spend more time planning than beginning writers. In one study, comparing prewriting time and total writing time of high school students, researchers found that their subjects spent a negligible fraction of their time planning, but experienced writers spend 65–85 percent of their writing time on the planning stage (Tate/Corbett 128–140).

When students tell you that they have difficulty meeting the page-length requirement or that they are having trouble organizing their ideas, give them some advice about planning. Remind them that planning doesn't necessarily mean sitting at the desk making notes, although it is a good idea to have paper and pen handy when you are thinking about a writing task. Some people plan their papers when they are taking a walk or sitting through a boring lecture. I do my best planning for writing projects in airports and doctors' offices. These are places where I am trying to block out the environment: thinking about a writing project is a very effective way of passing the time.

Drafting

Drafting, sometimes called "recording," "implementing," "writing," or "transcribing," is the process of "transforming meaning from one form of symbolization (thought) into another form of symbolization (graphic representation)" (Homes 208), or, said differently, it is the "spontaneous production of written prose" (Lytle). Often the writer is working from notes or an outline, but even if this is not the case, she is thinking about paragraphing, sentence form, and word choice. Drafting makes great demands on the [novice] writer, who might also be thinking about spelling, punctuation, organization, and clarity, at the same time he is trying to translate his thinking on the page (Scarmadelia et al. 52). We know that experienced writers have made some of these skills automatic, and therefore have less difficulty drafting than do beginning writers. For example, they need not worry about how to write grammatically correct sentences but instead can focus on other issues, such as organizing the content of their messages. They also have the ability to withhold some concerns for the revision stage, such as how to create a pleasing style while they concentrate on content.

As part of their research project, a group of writing tutors at La Salle asked students to describe their writing process. The tutors found that many of their peers do not spend hours drafting a paper, even if they have the time to do so before starting the final copy. Furthermore, the students interviewed claimed that they were writing their papers only once. Angela Balsamo, writing tutor, said, "I should understand that as a tutor I am probably reading a first draft that has been written hurriedly just to hand it in on time. This is because students are not accustomed to putting much thought or efforts into drafts." Perhaps students feel the strains of drafting, described by the researchers, and avoid the discomfort involved in drafting by giving this stage of the writing process short shrift.

Revision and Editing

Because most students seeking help from a writing tutor will have a draft or a partial draft in hand, revision is the stage of the writing process where you can have the most impact. Nancy Sommers makes a useful distinction between *revision* and *editing*. "Revision usually refers to reconsidering the larger elements of an essay, its content, development, and organization, whereas editing often refers to the processes by which the writer corrects what he or she has written, focusing chiefly on sentence correctness, spelling, usage and punctuation" (Tate/Corbett 122). Revision and editing, as research has demonstrated, are part of the writing process, from the moment we start to write (for example Perl). Experienced writers are always revising. I'm sure you have had the experience of changing a sentence, soon after you write it the first time. Writing using a word processor clearly encourages revision.

Once a first draft is completed, revision takes on new meaning. Experienced writers start reviewing their drafts for holistic issues such as organization and development of their ideas. Yet, in a study by the National Assessment for Educational Progress which periodically tests the writing abilities of students aged 9, 13, and 17, when students were asked to write for a given period of time and then rewrite for another given period of time, "approximately 90 percent of the students did nothing during the rewrite time. Only five percent of the few who tried to revise their writing improved their writing to a measurable degree; another five percent downgraded their writing to a measurable degree; all other students who attempted revision made no measurable change in their writing. This data holds true across age levels. and into the college years" (Weaver and Smith 44).

It is important to realize that even good students are often reluctant to revise. Here are some of the reasons.

Revision means punishment

Erika Lindemann in her widely acclaimed book on teaching college writing, *A Rhetoric for Writing Teachers*, points out that "For most students rewriting is a dirty word. They see it as punishment, as penalty for writing poorly in the first place." She says "many teachers reinforce this notion by insisting that students correct mistakes in papers already graded or complete workbook exercises on writing problems in someone else's prose" (172). For these students a suggestion from the tutor "to start from scratch" may mean they have failed the assignment.

However, even when students have a chance to revise before receiving a grade, their teacher's expectations strongly influence their approach. You can help change students' perceptions of "rewriting-as-punishment" and encourage the "view that rewriting remains crucial to the composing process, not an afterthought" (Lindemann 172). Donald Murray says that revision in the writing process is like kneading in the process of making bread. It's simply what one does; it is a natural part of the writing process. If you are assigned to a composition course where students are taught to revise, or, for that matter, any course where it is encouraged, you may find that students have positive views about revision.

Faculty can help you make the case for the importance of revision. Marc Moreau, who teaches philosophy at La Salle, tells his students that they should consider the writing tutors to be coaches in the writing process. His hand-out to students reminds them that the writing tutors are there to "help make effective revisions and to identify those features of [students'] prose that would likely cause disorientation, incomprehension, and understanding on the part of the reader."

Negative attitudes about revision are related to receiving poor grades

In a recent study, "The Role of Classroom Context in the Revision Strategies of Student Writers," in which Robert Yagelski asked the question "Do specific instructional features affect student revisions?" he discovered that despite a classroom characterized by process-oriented instruction, a writing program in which the teacher encouraged prewriting exercises, multiple drafts, and peer editing, what seemed to matter most was not how students were being taught to write, but the teacher's grading practices. If teachers base their grades on sentence level issues, students will continue to confine revision to the sentence (30). Writing tutors' discussions with students confirmed Yagelski's findings. One writing tutor said,

> The only evaluative criteria listed in Teacher X's 'Guidelines for Papers' mentioned proper construction, spelling, grammar, and punctuation. His students made a lot of basic errors. A conversation with Teacher X led me to believe that he saw the writing tutors as primarily satisfying the purpose of making sure that assignments could be evaluated more on the basics of mechanics than ideas. Perhaps because they knew that Teacher X cared more about mechanics, instead of ideas, the students were more responsive to conversations about grammar during our conferences that they were about possibilities for organizing their ideas. (Victoria Franz)

Victoria also reported that students came back for a second conference when their teacher said that their grade was penalized "mainly because of spelling and grammar mistakes." You can be sure that this student will confine revision to correcting errors in the future! On the other hand, Steve Martin, another writing tutor, says, "Because of Dr. Moreau's instruction to his class about our role, I believe that students approached conferences with the belief that we serve to aid the revision process, not to write the papers."

Revision means more work

The greatest stumbling block for most writers when it comes to revision is that it's hard work. Every sentence requires effort. To actually delete any of those sentences, after all of the effort that went into crafting them, is too painful. We hate to delete what took so much trouble to write in the first place. As I wrote the draft of this book, although I kept reminding myself that it was only a first draft, I kept secretly and illogically hoping that it would be the last. Maybe just this one time, I would strike it rich. No such luck. I have rewritten this chapter three times as of this morning, and will probably rewrite it again. If you discuss the times when you have been reluctant to revise with students, you will assure your tutees that they are in good company if they find revision painful.

One of my favorite stories about students' reluctance to revise involves a perplexed freshman I taught quite a few years ago. When reviewing Jodi's draft (not her real name) I remarked, "Jodi, either the first paragraph or the second paragraph probably needs to be eliminated. They seem to be about different subjects." She did not answer me at first, but just stared at her paper. I mistakenly thought she was trying to decide what she wanted to say in her essay, but, when she finally looked up, she said, "Well, I guess I will keep the second paragraph because it is longer." My student could not bear to part with too many of her hard-earned sentences.

Revision requires remembering the purpose
and audience of writing

A writer's response to his writing is very much conditioned by what he has already written. We fall in love with our own words and it is hard to see the material from the point of view of the audience. As Flower and Hayes have demonstrated, reseeing the material from the reader's perspective requires much practice. Writing my first grant proposal to the National Endowment for the Humanities, a government agency which funds faculty development programs among its other projects, taught me this lesson. My coauthor and I were surprised when, after sending a draft of the proposal for review to the Endowment, the program officer made extensive recommendations for revising the proposal. When we originally submitted the proposal we were very confident that it was in good shape. It took us several weeks before we were able to admit that we had to revise to meet the requirements of the NEH audience.

For students, remembering the purpose and the audience for the paper means constantly returning to the writing assignment, rereading the assignment, and a revising if some of what they have written is irrelevant to the assignment.

Revisions mean coming face to face with the "beast in the jungle"

Beginning writers often do not like to read their own writing. They often say, "I'm such a bad writer, I hate to read my own writing," or "My first draft is the best I can do. I can't improve it." This is when they need lots of reassurance about their writing. You should try to undo their negative attitudes towards their writing ability, possibly developed as a result of many past failures. One of my students, commenting about his high school writing experience said, "I felt that expectations were too high and that I could never be a good writer." Students will not reread their papers if they believe that their writing is terrible to begin with and beyond help.

Students' concepts of revision

Under the best of circumstances, assuming that students are willing to revise, research demonstrates that students' rewriting strategies are very different from those of experienced writers. The landmark essay on this topic, "Revision Strategies of Student Writers and Experienced Writers," should be required reading for all writing tutors. Nancy Sommers found that students see rewriting primarily as rewording. They worry about repetition. She calls this the "thesaurus" philosophy of writing: "The students consider the thesaurus a harvest of lexical substitutions and believe that most problems in their essays can be solved by rewording" (381). They delete or substitute words more often than they add them or reorder the material.

My own experience teaching writing supports Sommers' findings. Somewhere along the educational road, students learn to fear wordiness and repetition of the same word. They sometimes tell me that their grades were reduced if they exceeded the page limit, not only in high school but also in their college courses. Now I'm not one to beat up on high school teachers: I was one myself. Perhaps teachers, who are over-burdened with too many students, as is the case in many high schools, resort to this technique to cut down on the number of pages they must read. The fear of repeating the same word is harder to explain. This concern may be related to the popular but misguided idea that all writing

must sound "original." While there it is true that some teachers emphasize "creativity," students take it to the extreme. They consult their electronic thesauruses and often come up with synonyms not appropriate
for what they are trying to say. I might as well warn you; this is a very
hard habit to break.

The Effect of Attitude on the Composing Process

While early research focused on the stages of the composing process,
more recent studies attempt to understand the role that emotion and
motivation play in the writing process. To some extent, we have discussed the motivation issue within the context of social constructionist
theory, but Linda Cleary looked at motivation and attitude from the
perspective of emotion. Cleary based her investigations on the work of
psychologists and educators, not necessarily concerned with writing,
who have studied the effect of emotion and the ability to concentrate on
overall student performance. Her study included 40 male and female
11th graders representing different ethnic groups and different levels of
writing ability. She sought answers to these questions: "Why do most
teachers report that by eleventh grade most students resist writing?" and
"How do emotions connected with the context of writing interact with
the writing process?"

Cleary interviewed students, observed them in their classrooms, and
had them write several assignments using the *compose aloud* method that
requires students to explain what they are thinking and feeling when
they are writing. In her interviews she asked such questions as "What
has writing been like for you from the time you first remember until the
present? What do you remember of writing before you began school?
How did you learn to write? Tell me about a time when writing was
really good or bad for you. What is writing like for you now? Tell me as
many stories about writing as you can." She based these questions on
the assumption that since writing requires an enormous amount of
conscious attention, factors that inhibit concentration underlie students'
unwillingness to engage in the writing process and affect the way they
go about the process.

When threat enters the learning environment students cannot fully
use their cognitive processes. The student concentrates on surviving, not
learning. Writing tutors at La Salle, as a result of several projects they
conducted as part of their training course in tutoring, have identified

motivation or apprehension as significant factors in the writing process. In one study, the tutors found that the subject matter itself may be a cause of anxiety. Students seem most apprehensive about writing in courses in philosophy and religion, two subjects they did not take in high school. In both subjects the texts are difficult to read. In another study on student attitude toward writing, they discovered that students are less motivated to write in core courses than in major-related courses. One tutor said,

> It was a revelation to me how important motivation is to writing. Lack of interest is never a factor I took into consideration. All of us had a few students who clearly put little effort into their papers for subjects, which did not hold their interest. Now I am toying with the idea of getting some background on the student. If I find a student who is not motivated, maybe I can engage him in a discussion about why this course is important to them and why they should care even if the class is outside their major. I still think that the best reason one can offer for making an effort in all classes is getting the most you can out of every class. I could explain how I have used the knowledge in my core courses in other courses and in my life in general. If they still do not care, maybe I can stress the importance of grades and how they can drag down an otherwise decent GPA. (Tom McAllister)

Josh Schneiderman, another writing tutor, tried a different approach. He says,

> I encountered several students who appeared to have the necessary tools for writing a good paper, but seemed to rush through the paper. One of these students told me that she had no interest in literature, so she did not start the paper until two hours before it was due. Of course, it's impossible to make students appreciate James Joyce if they are uninterested. On one occasion, I was able to point out something humorous in the story. This seemed to spark her interest.

Josh tried to make the material more interesting to the student. You may have some success with this technique, but I'm afraid that you might have a hard time finding humor in some authors!

It's also important to keep in mind that some students actually enjoy writing. Lauren Turner, a student in one of my literature courses, said, "Personally I enjoy writing papers. They are a chance to freely express myself on a topic that interests me. The only time papers become difficult is when we don't like the book or can't understand it."

Computers and the Composing Process

Most college students now write their papers on word processors. The big question is "Do word processors 'cancel out' the findings of previous research on students' approaches to writing?" Interestingly, the answer is "no." One would assume that because the word processor makes writing so much easier, students would be spending more time on each stage of writing: For some students word processing allows them to spend less time on the writing task!

Writing tutors at La Salle who worked on a research project designed to understand the effect of word processors on the writing process reported that students said they no longer spent much time "brainstorming" before they started to write. Because typing is so easy on a word processor, students may entertain the illusion that the computer will actually write the paper for them. I know that when I sit down at the keyboard a false sense of power overtakes me.

The writing tutors, who conducted this study, agreed that the most valuable article they found on the effect of the computer on writing is James V. Catano's "Computer Based Writing: Navigating the Fluid Text." According to Catano, the fluid text is infinitely mutable and highly accommodating to writers because it helps them envision the paper as a cohesive whole and eliminates time-consuming large-scale revisions. However, these benefits may be overshadowed for the novice writer. Instead, the fluid text may become an "unmanageable mess plagued by a lack of structure" (313).

Conclusion

Helping students modify their approach to writing is one of your biggest challenges. Gordon Rohman, writing about teaching composition in the 1960s, said, "Unless we can somehow introduce students to the dynamics of creation, we too often simply discourage their hopes of ever writing well" (106). Your task may not be to *introduce* students to the "dynamics of creation." Hopefully their teachers will do that. However, peer tutors can convince students that learning or practicing more effective methods for working through a writing assignment is one of the benefits of peer tutoring. These questions may help you encourage students to *take stock* of their approach to writing. If you can engage a student in a discussion about her approach to writing, you may be able to share some *words of wisdom* from the research on the writing process and from the stock of writing methods that have worked for you! The result: less apprehension about writing, which may translate into the willingness to start a paper more than 24 hours before it's due!

Questions for Discussion and Writing

1. Answer the questions in this Writing Process Survey. After thinking about your approach to writing, would you like to modify that approach? If so, how?
   - How would you describe your present attitude towards writing?
   - What kinds of writing do you like to do most? Why?
   - Are you more comfortable writing for some courses rather than others? Why?
   - Describe your writing process. What percentage of time do you spend on the following stages of the process: planning, drafting, revising, editing?
   - Which stage of the process is the most difficult? Why?
   - How does using a word processor affect your approach to writing?
2. Write a brief essay (2–3 pages) on the topic "How I Learned to Write." Define what you mean by "learning to write." Who were the most important people in your writing autobiography—parents, teachers, friends, and so on? Which experiences were most significant: writing for courses, school publications, writing for yourself—for example diaries, poetry, and so on?
3. Read a book by an author who describes his development as a writer (for example, *Growing Up* by Russell Baker, *One Writer's Beginnings* by Eudora Welty). Summarize the writing process of the writer you choose.

Works Cited

Catano, James V. "Computer Based Writing: Navigating the Fluid Text." *College Composition and Communication* 36 (1985): 309–316.

Cleary, Linda Miller. *From the Other Side of the Desk: Students Speak Out About Writing*. Portsmouth, NH: Heinemann-Boynton/Cook, 1991.

Flower, Linda. "Writer Based Prose: A Cognitive Base for Problems in Writing." *College English* 41 (September 1979): 19–37.

Flower, Linda and John Hayes. "The Cognition of Discovery: Defining a Rhetorical Problem." *The Writing Teachers Sourcebook*. 2nd ed. Ed. Gary Tate and Edward Corbett. New York: Oxford University Press, 1988.

Glatthorn, Allan A. "The Teaching of Writing: A Review of Theory, Research, and Practice." Philadelphia, 1983. Unpublished materials.

Homes, Ann. "Research on the Composing Process." *Review of Educational Research* 53 (Summer, 1983): 201–216.

Lindemann, Erika. *Rhetoric for Writing Teachers*. 2nd ed. New York: Oxford University Press, 1987.

Lytle, Susan L. and Morton Botel. "The Pennsylvania Framework for Reading, Writing, and Talking Across the Curriculum." Harrisburg: The Pennsylvania Department of Education, 1990.

Perl, Sondra. "Understanding Composing." *Landmark Essays on the Writing Process*. Ed. Sondra Perl. Davis, CA: Hermagoras Press, 1994.

Rohmann, Gordon D. "Pre-Writing: The Stage of Discovery in the Writing Process." *College Composition and Communication* 16 (May, 1965): 106–112.

Scarmadelia, M., Cary Bereiter and Hillel Goelman. "What Writers Know: The Language Process and Structure of Written Discourse?" *The Role of Production Factors in Writing Ability*. Ed. Martin Nystrand. New York: Academic Press, 1982.

Sommers, Nancy. "Revision of Student Writers and Experienced Adult Writers." *The Writing Teachers Sourcebook*. 2nd ed. Ed. Gary Tate and Edward Corbett. New York: Oxford University Press, 1988.

Weaver, Francis and M. Lynn Smith. *Expressive Writing: A Workshop Manual*. Cincinatti, OH: Cincinnati Public Schools, 1985.

Yagelski, Robert. "The Role of Classroom Context in the Revision Strategies." *Research in the Teaching of English* 29 (May, 1995), 216–238.

For Further Reading

Joram, Elana, et al. "The Effects of Revising with a Word Processor on Writing Composition." *Research in Teaching English* 26:2 (1992): 167–193.

Perl, Sondra. Ed. *Landmark Essays on the Writing Process*. Davis, CA: Hermagoras Press, 1994.

Selfe, Cynthia and Susan Hillgoss. *The Complications of Teaching and Learning with Technology*. New York: MLA, 1994.

Walvoord, Barbara and Lucille McCarthy. *Thinking and Writing in College: A Naturalistic Study of Students in Four Disciplines*. Urbana, IL: NCTE, 1991.

6

Tutoring Special Students

Since the decade of the 1920s, when research on writing shifted to "the process through which children acquire competency or expressiveness in language," ideas related to the development of writing ability and the nature of the writing process have been strongly influenced by social factors effecting the students. In a sense the two theoretical strands which supported the "writing revolution," namely the cognitivist and the social constructionist viewpoints, have become increasingly integrated. For example, Shirley Brice Heath's research, often cited by composition theorists, indicates that "students' readiness to develop their writing in school is greatly influenced by their social and cultural backgrounds" (Bizzell 187). On the college level, the social aspects of learning how to write include the influence of age, race, class, and gender. In this chapter, I present the outlines of the theory and research related to tutoring (the so-called) "special students."

There is a great deal of truth to the statement "there is no such thing as the average student" when one is talking about the present-day college population. If you have been tutoring in the writing center at your school, you know that the distinction between the "traditional" and the "nontraditional" student is becoming meaningless. The person sitting next to you may be a "thirty something" student returning to school, a first-generation college student, or perhaps a student who has recently immigrated to America, or even a good student writer! Whether they form the majority or the minority of students at your school, each group comes with certain traits that should influence our tutoring practices.

This chapter will deal with five such student types:

1. The student who speaks a nonstandard form of English at home
2. The student for whom English is a second language
3. The student who lacks basic writing skills
4. The returning adult student
5. The "good" student writer.

You will be happy to know that there is no need to develop a new approach to tutoring for these students. Instead, we can build on our general tutoring strategies to accommodate the special traits of different students.

Nonstandard Dialect and ESL Students: Some Background and Definitions

The United States has the most heterogeneous population of any nation in the world. If you live in a large city you already know that. Just take a ride on a bus or subway train and look at your fellow passengers. If you live in the suburbs or a small town notice the newcomers on your block. One of my favorite activities when I visit my hometown, New York, is to ride the subway in Manhattan and try to guess the country of origin of the people sitting across from me. Impossible, but fun. It makes me proud to live in the United States. As I pointed out in a textbook I wrote several years ago, *Teaching Writing in Middle and Secondary Schools*, "large numbers of children in American schools either speak a dialect defined by region or ethnic group or a native language other than English" (89). This was certainly true of my mother, who arrived in New York in the 1920s from Eastern Europe. She recalls being embarrassed but proud when, asked to say her name in first grade, replied, "My *nomen* (Yiddish for name) is Esther Ebovitz." The class laughed, but the teacher scolded them and said, "Welcome to America, Esther." "Your *name* is Esther Abovitz." The teacher used the right approach. She modeled the correct way of saying the sentence, without criticizing my mom's use of the Yiddish word for *name* or correcting her pronunciation. We can learn from this teacher's approach, and also add the kind of instruction appropriate to college level students.

What is Standard American English?

Standard American English is the dialect of the American academic world and other institutions and businesses which require formal written English. Some composition specialists reserve the term *Standard American English* (SAE) for the spoken language and use the term *Edited American English* (EAE) to refer to writing. As Beth Neman, a composition scholar, says, "Even a white Scarsdale banker's everyday speech differs somewhat from the language the banker would write in a business or academic setting" (101).

No one speaks pure SAE all of the time. My mom was lucky. Many teachers might have responded, "Esther, your sentence is wrong. Use the English word for name and pronounce 'A' correctly." During the last 30 years we have become particularly sensitive to problems related to teaching SAE to students born in America who speak a dialect of English different from SAE and students who are struggling to learn English as a second language without implying that the dialect or language that they speak outside of school is inferior to SAE. For example, research shows that Black English Vernacular is not a "degenerative or ungrammatical version of the standard dialect, but a fully grammatical language in its own right with different grammatical rules different from those of SAE. It still maintains some of the features of West African languages that shaped its development." Black English Vernacular includes the

> habitual tense of the African languages which is not characteristic of Standard English but is expressed in Black English Vernacular by "be" ("He be coming," or "Mama be working"). Black English Vernacular also shares the West African avoidance of a double signification of plurality ("two dog"), a feature also of Chinese–American English derived from many of the Chinese languages. Black English Vernacular, like the Appalachian dialect, also retains features of the 16th and 17th century English spoken in Colonial America and immortalized in the King James Bible. Among these features are the repeated subject ("The boy, he [. . .]" as in "Thy rod and thy staff, they [. . .]") and the reinforced negative ("Nobody don't [. . .]"), commonplace in Shakespeare's plays. (Neman 275)

Standard American English is not superior to Black Vernacular Dialect. Both serve the communication needs of their speakers, and both have a rich vocabulary and systematic grammar. However, because SAE is the language used in government, business, and education, and is very similar to its written counterpart, EAE, students need to know it. As teachers we know that we must teach our students SAE without insisting that they give up the dialect which they speak at home and which is their link to their families and friends. Our goal is to introduce students to the idea of code switching, the ability to use the dialect appropriate for their communication needs in a given context.

In "Fostering Dialect Shift in African–American Students," an essay which appears in *Dynamics of the Writing Conference*, Susan Horn observes that as writers mature and begin to recognize the differences between dialects, they will make spontaneous shifts from their spoken dialect to EAE, if given enough time to write successive drafts. She says about her research,

> My findings reinforced my intuition that the students whom we see in our Midwestern university writing center are intelligent adults who are quite conscious that the dialect of the classroom and of writing is fairly close to the dialect they hear spoken on the evening news. These students are experts in switching styles when appropriate, for they will often say to a teacher a sentence such as "My sister is very considerate," and then promptly make an aside to a classmate such as "She don't be doing no work; she always be leaving it to me." Such students are capable of correcting many of their own errors if such errors are ignored until the appropriate stage of writing, which is editing. (105)

Horn quotes from an early draft of a paper, where the student wrote, "Mom, those kids alway [crossed out] just be trying to fake you out. They're not that nice." The final draft reads, "Mom, those kids are trying to fake you out; they're not nice." Horn says that at times students may have no choice but to rely on their native dialect to express certain ideas. She concludes, "As teachers and tutors, we must not gag the natural, outer manifestation of the students 'inner speech' before they have a chance to figure out what they want to say. We can always work on the fine points of Standard English later, after meaning has been established [...]" (108).

Implications for Tutoring

When you encounter papers with a pattern of incorrect verb forms follow the procedure suggested in Chapter 3. First focus on rhetorical issues which affect the quality of the whole paper. Because you may see the student only once, note the verb form errors, but see if the student can repair the errors independently during your conference. Regardless of the methods you choose to increase students' awareness of dialect interference in their writing, always remain aware of their feelings. Avoid words like *wrong* or *incorrect*, but instead use words like *inappropriate*. One technique for emphasizing the value of nonstandard dialects is to give students the opportunity to tell you about the features of the dialect they speak at home or with friends.

The Student for Whom English is a Second Language

Everyone has a hobby. Mine is the study of Hebrew. I've been at it for quite some time. I began studying it in high school and college. Then there was a long hiatus, when I neither studied the language nor spoke it. But, several years ago, a friend invited me to attend a Hebrew class offered in our neighborhood. Needless to say, I was a tad rusty. However, after a year of reentry I was able to read and speak simple Hebrew. Writing—well that was another matter, and five years later, my writing in Hebrew lags way behind my ability to speak and read. My brief essays in Hebrew are returned to me with much red ink, especially when I use prepositions and idioms. Studying a foreign language is a humbling experience! As a writing tutor, especially when you are reading a paper written by an *ESL* student, think about your own experience learning a foreign language, whether in high school or college.

Students for whom English is a second language (ESL) share some of the same problems of students who speak nonstandard dialects. However, nonstandard dialect speakers already know (or have been told about) the fundamental rules of sentence forms in English. In contrast, ESL speakers must make the transfer from languages based on grammatical features not typical of English. This example, from the *Bedford Guide for Writing Tutors*, illustrates the differences between a Korean sentence and English sentence:

> English: Last night, I ate rice instead of bread.
> Korean: Yesterday evening in rice instead of bread ate. (Ryan 43)

However, despite the difficulties of learning a new language, the ESL student is not hampered by the psychological barriers encountered by students who speak nonstandard dialects. Foreign-born students usually do not have feelings of inferiority about their language, but may be facing other psychological barriers resulting from being unaccustomed to experiencing difficulty in school (Soven 9). Furthermore, the ESL instructor must be aware of cultural differences, especially as they pertain to schooling. In *The Bedford Guide for Writing Tutors* Leigh Ryan offers some suggestions which apply to both classroom instruction and one-on-one tutoring of ESL students:

> When you tutor someone from a similar background to yours, you will both think and behave in similar ways; however, differences, especially in the areas of interpersonal and written communication may become apparent when you tutor someone from a different culture or subculture. For example, in some cultures questioning authority is frowned upon, and you may find students who are reluctant to ask you a question, to admit they don't understand something. The amount of personal space people desire differs among cultures, and you may tutor students who make you feel uncomfortably crowded as you work together. Whatever differences you encounter, it is important to treat each student with respect and sensitivity.
>
> Likewise, acceptable ways of presenting information differ among cultures. Americans tend to value the direct approach, but some cultures believe that meaning should be implied rather than spelled out directly. Still others approach a problem by giving its detailed history first, information that we might find unnecessary. We need to recognize such differences as cultural and explain appropriate rhetorical patterns in English. (44)

The recommendations below are based on Ryan's suggestions (44–45):

- Give directions plainly. Watch students' expressions and ask questions to see if they comprehend explanations. If you are not sure whether a student understands something you've said, ask him or her to explain what you have said or to give you an example.
- If a student doesn't understand a comment or explanation, rephrase it. Don't raise your voice or simply repeat the same words.
- If you have difficulty understanding an ESL student, watch for facial expressions as he or she speaks. The combination of saying and hearing can help you to follow what the student is saying.
- Many ESL students write better than they speak [although they may be the exception]. Don't assume that because you have trouble understanding a student's speech, he or she will have problems with their writing.
- Do not feel compelled to give the grammatical explanation of constructions you are teaching the student. Many foreign students are accustomed to imitation as a form of instruction. You can help

students rephrase a sentence and produce other sentences of the same kind. Producing such examples establishes patterns that students can begin to incorporate into their writing and their speaking.

Two peer tutors at La Salle developed a checklist which demonstrates at a glance some of the differences between tutoring students whose first language is English and ESL writers. The tutors incorporate many of Leigh Ryan's suggestions, and also presents another view on some issues. Can you identify the differences between Ryan's suggestions and the peer tutors' approach?

Approach for First Language Writers	Approach for ESL Writers
Indirect tutoring (Socratic method)	Direct tutoring
Tutor lets student do all the writing	Tutor informs and collaborates with student about problems and possible solutions
Student talks through what she is trying to say	Student has difficulty talking through the ideas and may be more comfortable with the written language
Tutor gives students strategies for editing and proofing her paper	Tutor often helps to edit paper
Student reads her work aloud to find sentence problems	Tutor points out problems and explains how to fix them

Tips for Tutors of ESL Students

- Modify your resources. Use a simple dictionary instead of a college level dictionary.
- Brush up on your grammar. Although you don't need to be an expert, many ESL students want deeper explanations of how and why grammar works.
- Watch for nuances. Sometimes ESL students get words from the dictionary which will have peculiar connotations in their papers.

- Watch for plagiarism. This doesn't necessarily happen on purpose. In some cultures borrowing from other sources is accepted.
- Give equal amounts of sympathy and encouragement. ESL students deal with more than just writing.
- Rephrase comments that confuse students. If the student doesn't get what you are trying to say, try rephrasing your comments instead of repeating yourself.
- Notice students' expressions and body language. As with any other tutee, body language helps you see if the students are confused.
- Be patient. You will probably need to devote more time to an ESL student because you will need to explain things more thoroughly. (Cech and McCarthy)

This section should end with not only a note of encouragement but also a warning not to expect too much. Marilyn Sternglass, author of *Time to Know Them: A Longitudinal Study of Writing and Learning on the College Level* (1997), reports that "second dialect and second language students benefit most strongly from opportunities to revise and edit." They often know the rules, but when writing they suffer from cognitive overload. Often they can improve their drafts when given the chance. Sternglass also says that "some features of second language development can be acquired only over time, particularly tense accuracy, subject–verb agreement, and correct use of plurals" (24). The plight of a former student, who took several courses with me, illustrates this very clearly.

Taka Kumazawa is from Japan. When he came to La Salle, his ability to speak English was impressive. He had spent a year in high school in Philadelphia before entering La Salle. However, his writing skills were weak. I was more than perplexed by his first essay in my composition class. At the time I knew very little about the writing of ESL students, especially about how to deal with their numerous grammatical errors, particularly with prepositions. I did not know how to get Taka to write paragraphs that were longer than three or four sentences, or how to help him master many of the idiomatic expressions in English—just a few of the challenges I faced. However, Taka had a lot going for him. Although he was on the swimming team, which took up lots of his time, his determination was indomitable. We made a contract. I would read his drafts as often as he was willing to resubmit them, on the condition that he also visit the writing center regularly. Taka came to my office in the mornings after swim practice, afternoons during his lunch hour, and sometimes late in the day before I left for home.

I guess I wasn't surprised when he reappeared in one of my literature courses in the next semester, and then in yet another of my courses the semester after that. No doubt he was making progress, but the going was slow, especially on the sentence level. By the time he was a senior, he had mastered the organization and development patterns of academic discourse, but his sentences, although longer and more complex than those he wrote as a freshman, still exhibited problems related to his faulty use of English grammar and usage. When he registered for the course which trains students interested in teaching English on the high school level, I was a bit taken aback. He announced that his goal was to return to Japan and teach English. Could Taka progress to the point where he could teach English to others? When I last heard from Taka, he reported that he was doing well in a Master of Arts program pursuing his goal to become a teacher of English in Japan!

Of course, you will most likely not have the opportunity to work with an ESL student over a period of several years, but my experience teaching and tutoring Taka should be encouraging. ESL students do progress slowly. Be patient, and you will enjoy working with them.

The Student Who Lacks Basic Writing Skills

I keep in my files a small folder of student papers that go back ten years in my teaching career. They are the first papers I ever read by severely under prepared freshman writer, and I remember clearly the day I received them. The students who wrote the papers were then enrolled in the SEEK program for poverty area youth which preceded Open Admissions at City College and served in many ways as the model for the skills programs that were to be developed under that policy.

I remember sitting alone in the worn urban classroom where my students had just written their first essays and where now I began to read them, hoping to be able to assess quickly the sort of task that lay ahead of us that semester. But the writing was so stunningly unskilled that I could not begin to define the task nor even sort out the difficulties. I could only sit there, reading and rereading the alien papers, wondering what had gone wrong and trying to understand what I at this eleventh hour of my students' lives could do about it. (Shaughnessy, *Errors and Expectations: A Guide for the Teacher of Basic Writing*)

With these words, Mina Shaughnessy began the conversation about teaching writing to the "basic writer," the student whose writing exhibits a wide range of characteristics not typical of the average college student. The basic writer is not simply defined by the number of sentence level errors in his papers. For example, in "The Content of Basic Writers Essays" Andrea Lunsford explains that "basic writers tend to focus on personal content, using it as conclusive evidence, or they evaluate abstract questions solely in terms of personal effects; they rely on clichéd maxims in place of generalizations; they see themselves as passive victims of authority; and use stylistic features such as personal pronouns that reflect these content characteristics" (Bizzel et al. 153). In *Errors and Expectations*, Shaugnessy devotes Chapters 1–5 to students' problems with handwriting, punctuation, syntax, and spelling. But in Chapters 6–8 she shows that basic writers are unfamiliar with the concepts and argument forms of academic writing. Chapter 7, "Beyond the Sentence," is a "must read" for just about everyone who teaches writing, not just peer tutors. Shaughnessy's discussion about the inability of basic writers to move up and down the ladder of abstraction between generalizations and specifics helps us to understand the reason that many students, not just basic writers, have trouble with the conventions of academic argumentation.

By now you may be thinking that many of the papers you review are characterized by the errors Shaughnessy and Lunsford identify as the characteristics of the basic writer. You are correct. Keep in mind the words of James Kinneavy, a famous scholar of rhetoric: "All categories leak." When we try to fit writers into neat categories, invariably they overlap. However, the basic writer is distinguished from the average writer, sometimes by the frequency of errors on the sentence level, and at other times by the extent of the gap between her approach to writing an argument in contrast to the average writer. Basic writers may have more problems in one area of writing than another.

For example, some basic writers have complex sentence problems. Sternglass provides this example of basic writing in a paper written for a women's studies course. Although the student, Linda, had cited research in the body of her paper, the essay concludes:

> I, overall, have shown just a microcosm of women's problems from assorted viewpoints. Women have suffered in this world of ours. Unfortunately, women's cries go unanswered. As human beings we should teach our society to understand the plight of women's hardships just as we thoroughly study the plight of others. People should be taught about women and their struggle to cope in a rampantly sexist society. Showing people daily experiences of what women go through will not only open their eyes, but it will give them a better sense of understanding the women who incorporate their lives. Today,

nothing could be more vital for a woman and also a man. Once we establish a basis for equilibrium between the sexes, the better the future will start to hold for them.

Linda's instructor wrote "A good start, but you really don't give enough attention to the kinds of evidence that support your very important insights" (Sternglass 193). Although this student's sentences are for the most part grammatically correct, this student has much to learn about the kinds of evidence required for the argument in an academic paper.

On the other hand, this paper is riddled with error on the sentence level. The student tries to explain the reasons for a judge deciding that the Community Decency Act is unconstitutional.

> The Community Decency ACT in 1996, is suppose to protect the children from the explicit world of cyberspace. Because the Act did not live up to its standards; Stewart Dalzell, a federal based judge in Philadelphia, made the right decision to put an end to the Community Decency Act. Judge Dalzell decides that the Community Decency Act is unconstitutional because it fails to protect the children's innocence, it violates the First Amendment's right to freedom of speech and it overrides parent's authority.

Sternglass says, "as work became harder, this student was unable to write." I don't know if this is really a writing problem or not. The teacher commented, in response to this student's paper, "While your paper is well organized, it has many difficulties such as mistakes in citation and major errors in diction" (Sternglass 286).

Tutoring the Basic Writer: Strategies

Many of the strategies recommended for the ESL and second dialect student are appropriate when tutoring basic writers. Shaughnessy and others recommend trying to identify a "pattern of error," instead of seeing each mistake as discrete (13). This is good advice for tutoring all kinds of students, but especially important when tutoring basic writers.

In addition, try to understand the reasons for the errors, especially if your tutee is willing to talk with you about her writing experience in the past. The reasons basic writers have problems may be less obvious than the explanation for errors in the papers of ESL students and students who write in a nonstandard dialect. Error analysis, a method long used for understanding error in reading and second language learning and now being applied to writing, offers several explanations for why errors occur. David Bartholomae wrote one of the first essays on applying error analysis to teaching writing. In "The Study of Error" he says,

> Error analysis begins with a theory of writing, a theory of language develop-ment that allows us to see errors as evidence of choice or strategy among a range of possible choices or strategies. They provide evidence of an indi-vidual style of using language and making it work; they are not a simple record of what the writer failed to do because of incompetence or indiffer-ence. Errors are seen as necessary stages of an individual's development and as data that provide insight into idiosyncratic strategies of a particular language user at a particular point in his [her] language acquisition. They are not simply "noise in the system." (quoted in Graves 315)

Error analysis assumes that most errors are developmental; students either do not have the knowledge to identify the error, or they are follow-ing a system of writing they have invented but one at odds with the con-ventions of academic writing. A lack of writing instruction in elementary and secondary school may have contributed to this developmental lag. Another possibility is that the kind of writing instruction students received did not prepare them for writing in college. For example, when I pointed out that she needed more evidence from the short story that was the subject of her paper, one of my students said, "Oh, I was told to be cre-ative, to put more of my own opinions in my papers."

Students with Learning Disabilities

Sometimes students will be very candid and admit that they have a learning disability. It's becoming more acceptable to acknowledge learn-ing deficits, and students are more willing to discuss their learning prob-lems, if they are aware of them, than they were in the past. The term *learning disability* encompasses a wide range of learning disorders; how-ever, whatever the cause, these students usually have problems "per-ceiving and processing" information (Ryan 45). The catchall phrase "learning disability" is often used to describe very different kinds of problems, such as difficulty reading college level materials, or the inabil-ity to organize information logically. Many learning disabilities are mild and allow you to use the same techniques that are appropriate for all writers who need special help. However, once you realize that you are not successful with a writer who has an acknowledged learning disabil-ity, you should refer the student to the trained professional on campus who knows how to deal with learning problems. (See the For Further Reading section for materials on learning disabilities.)

The Returning Student

As returning students become a larger fraction of the college population, research on methods for teaching adult learners continues to grow. Our experience at La Salle with returning students has confirmed the findings of much of this research. On the positive side, these students often have certain strengths that help them write their papers. Because of their maturity and experience in the work world, they often bring a very disciplined and organized approach to their writing. However, on the negative side, many adult learners, in addition to being rusty (they haven't written an academic paper in many years), lack confidence when it comes to writing assignments. This is especially true if they have been working in a profession which requires very little writing. In *Transitions*, a book about returning students, William Bridges says that "every transition begins with an ending. When people go back to school there is an anxiety associated with 'starting over'" (105). In her essay, "Experts with Life, Novices with Writing," Marcia Hurlow gives some excellent advice for working with the adult writers. She says,

> Considering whether students' insecurity stems from fear of being evaluated or from fear of being rejected as a person makes it possible to design appropriate approaches for particular students. More importantly, knowing whether students' problems with writing stem from a lack of competence with language or from an inability to tap fully their competence because of insecurity can make a difference in what is taught. (68)

I would add, "and how it is taught." For example, tutors must take great care to not "talk down" to older students.

At La Salle, writing tutors have had very few problems working with adult learners. We receive more requests for undergraduate writing tutors than we can fill from faculty who teach in our graduate and continuing study programs. Their courses include the largest number of adult learners at La Salle because most courses in these programs are held in the evening. When I first ask writing tutors if they are interested in working with these students, few volunteer. They can't imagine tutoring older students. Typically I assign experienced tutors to these classes, not because beginning tutors don't have the skills to work with them, but just as the adult learners lack confidence, so do beginning tutors. If you are a novice tutor you may be somewhat apprehensive about your ability to help your peers, but even more apprehensive about your ability to help an older student. For example, Angela Balsalmo, a writing tutor, says,

> I really admire and respect people who come back to school after having been away for years. I usually take a night class every semester, so I am often in a class with nontraditional students. I find that they are usually much more organized and conscientious than traditional students. They have a lot on their plate, and they can juggle everything well. I enjoy having nontraditional students in my class because they motivate me to work harder, and because their contributions to class discussions often bring more insight and worldly knowledge to the discussion than my fellow classmates.
>
> However, I think I would be nervous to the point of not functioning if I had to try to tell someone significantly older than myself that he had to make changes to improve his paper. I do think, though, that if both the student and I could get past the awkwardness of the situation, he or she would probably be more receptive to my help than traditional students.

Angela is right. Adult learners welcome the assistance of student tutors. Most have no problem working with students who in some cases are the same age as their sons and daughters. The tutors are usually more ill at ease than the tutees at their first conference. However, tutors consistently say, much to their surprise, that the adult students are often very friendly and extremely willing to accept their help. The instructors also report back favorably. Dr. Janice Beitz, an instructor in the School of Nursing, has great praise for the writing tutors, after having worked with them for more than 10 years. She says, "The tutor gives the student a non-threatening read and an incentive to fix problem papers. The tutors are terrific."

Tutors who are themselves adult learners can be very successful with this population. Our own experience at La Salle supports Hurlow's conclusion: "Older tutors of the same gender who have had similar experiences in returning to college have been invaluable for these nontraditional students" (69). It's not often that returning students apply to become writing tutors. However, occasionally I get lucky. Cynthia Finley Barry, a Writing Fellow at La Salle several years ago, had worked as an editor for a large publishing house prior to returning to school. Cynthia was amazingly effective with the adult students in our nursing program. They adored her.

My advice to writing tutors who tutor adults: Begin by asking some questions to "break the ice." Demonstrating an interest in the adult student's career is often a good way to start. If, like Angela Balsalmo, you have been in classes with adult learners and your feelings are similar to hers about their contribution to the class, you might indicate that while you are eager to tutor adult learners, you are somewhat ill at ease. This is another way of establishing a relationship with your tutee, who will most likely try to assure you that she is looking forward to your help.

Some more advice: At La Salle we have found that adult learners have little patience with some of the tutoring strategies we use with traditional age college students. Adult learners often want very comprehensive reviews of their errors. Most of them have a much greater tolerance for "red ink" than traditional age undergraduates. They assume that you are the expert when it comes to writing, and they are highly motivated to act on your suggestions. There is one pitfall: Be careful to remind them that you are not in fact an expert and that there may be problems in their papers that you have overlooked. Also, keep in mind that because they often lack confidence, they may be overly negative about their writing. When you praise certain characteristics of their essays, they are often disbelieving, but encouraged!

The Good Student Writer

Perhaps the biggest surprise of your peer-tutoring experience will show up in the writing center in the form of the "good student writer." It's easy to assume that the only students who come to a writing center are poor writers. Unfortunately, that assumption is often correct. Although all writing centers advertise that they welcome all students, and that all students can benefit from another pair of eyes when revising, it is indeed true that good student writers, students who usually receive a "B" or better on their papers, may visit the writing center only to get help on special writing projects, such as resumes. If you are a tutor in a curriculum based peer tutoring program (a Writing Fellows program) where everyone in a particular course must submit their drafts to a writing tutor, you may be surprised at the number of good writers in the course.

Writing tutors often don't know what to do with a draft that is already in the "B" range except to search for grammar and punctuation errors. Such papers are relatively free of egregious errors—so what's next?

Let's take the same approach we used to think about the needs of other "special" writers. First, let's try to understand the student who writes well. We need to ask the question, "What is this student hoping to accomplish through the writing assignment?" Good student writers usually know that they can write a competent paper and receive at least a "B." Once they are liberated from worrying about the grade, they have the opportunity to develop other objectives for their writing assignments.

My research on good student writers involved a study of students in a philosophy class who typically received "A"s on their papers. These remarks, by two students, Mike and Penny, are similar to the comments of the other "A" students in the study when I asked them about their goals for writing assignments.

> Mike: He [the instructor] wants you to know the material, what Augustine said (I really like the papers on St. Augustine.) because it's so important. We try to get inside his [Augustine's] head. He wants you to know each philosopher, where he plugs in [. . .] He is trying to get us to enter something—to really get behind what is being said [. . .] I guess I'm writing for the instructor, but for me it's always personal. I try to see how I can use the material to make my own decisions [. . .] Just formulating the material myself with the notes, with the material we talked about in class seems to give it a different angle [. . .] It takes me a long time; it involves a lot of creative writing. (14)

> Penny: Because the questions for these assignments are not trivial, it permits people to interpret them differently. If you have an interesting question, there are lots of ways into it. People can interpret it differently. I perceive myself as struggling to simply get a tiny grasp of an immense problem so you can talk about it in an intelligible way. Reading, lectures, and class discussions are intimately related, but you need to figure out those relationships and express them in your paper. The three page limit forces you to think and writer clearly. He only wants 3–5 pages on extremely complex questions. You need to be very concise, and that's part of his purpose in limiting the paper to only 3–5 pages. It really puts the pressure on you to think clearly.
>
>   You know how you are supposed to end papers by restating the question [. . .] but I never do that. If your paper is very good, it does not matter. He [the professor] wants to see that you are grappling with the subject [. . .] wrestling with it. It's got to be in the paper. I think the structure is secondary; but as one gets to understand the issue, it takes care of itself. It [the structure] could even get in the way of the idea if it doesn't follow from the content. (14)

Notice the similarities in Mike's and Penny's responses. Both see the writing assignment as an opportunity to learn the course material. They focus on the importance of understanding the question. Both view writing as a creative act—the creation of something new even if the assignment requires synthesizing materials from class, the text, and lectures. Mike also views each opportunity to write as personal. He views writing in the philosophy class as an opportunity to apply philosophy to his life. Penny views the writing assignment as an opportunity to practice thinking clearly. One of her most interesting comments is the comment in which she says that the page limit forces her to think clearly.

If we use Penny and Mike as exemplars of good student writers, then what are the implications for tutoring good student writers? Their comments liberate writing tutors from the idea that all you can do for a good writer is to make some stylistic suggestions and help them repair the few grammatical errors that may be present in their papers. Writing tutors need to go beyond the surface when reading good papers. Assume that the paper of a good student writer includes a clear thesis statement, has ideas organized logically and arguments developed with sufficient reasons and examples. The paper begins with an introduction and ends with a conclusion. Here are some suggestions for working with the good draft just described:

- Ask the student about his goals for writing the assignment. What is he trying to accomplish (for example, understand the material, write a paper that is original, and so on)? Once you understand the student's goals, you can then ask the student if he thinks he has accomplished them.
- Ask the student about possible interpretations of the assignment. Check to see if the student made a conscious effort to examine these possible interpretations.
- Ask the student if he or she can think of other possible strategies for making his or her paper even more effective, such as improving the quality of the argument by a more thorough analysis of the texts which are the subject of the paper.
- Check for the clarity of the argument. For example, read the paper for coherence. In other words, the ideas may be logically organized, but are the relationships between the ideas clear? This quality often distinguishes "A" papers from "B" papers.
- Check the paper for style and error.

If you adopt this approach, you will also help to change the attitudes of good student writers toward the role of peer tutors. You will give them the incentive to revise good papers into excellent papers!

Conclusion

My primary message in this chapter is that you can follow the same guidelines for tutoring special students that you use for helping most students. However, no two students are alike. You must constantly modify your peer-tutoring technique to meet the special needs of different groups of students as well as individual students. This chapter tries to help you accomplish that aim.

Questions for Discussion and Writing

1. Quan Trieu is an ESL student in La Salle's Academic Discovery Program, a program for freshmen who do not fully meet La Salle University's entrance requirements, but who are admitted because they show extraordinary potential. This paper was written in the summer course for students admitted into this program. At the end of the course, Quan's teacher, Dr. Marjorie Allen, wrote, "Quan has major ESL reading and writing issues, but she works very hard and is the most determined and disciplined student in the class. Quan worked hard on her corrections. She knows most rules, but can't always apply them to correct her essays. She has trouble with agreement, word endings, and makes modification errors."

   Quan's class was asked to write about the interests of one of their classmates.

   Using the techniques recommended for tutoring ESL students, respond to this paper below in writing and in a mock conference in which another tutor plays Quan.

   Tia Johnson's Interests

   Tia Johnson is one of La Salle's ADP student who is interests to know why she is attending La Salle and how she will adapts to her new environments. In Tia's colleges research, she found out La Salle is one of the best business school University in Philadelphia. Therefore, that was one main reason why she will be attending La Salle in this fall and majoring in Economic. Another reason is she believed in her gut feeling, she said, "My gut gave her the courage to try out La Salle." Lastly, she like the diversity La Salle had created. She believed "one can't knows his/her potential unless his or she interacts and learns from different people who has open minds; so the person becomes a better well rounded person." She majors in economic because she wants to learn more about the economy and how unemployment affects the business's world such as restaurants and malls (for instant). The Gov't/Consumer class she took during her senior year in High School also got her interested in the business field. One of the outside activities Miss Johnson enjoys doing is playing computer game named Sims because she can builds and create her own house and family. The clubs she is planning to get involves in La Salle are the Investment Club because she considers herself as a good saver and likes to discuss how other invest his/her money. Another club that interested her is the Student Economic Club, because is related to her major and she hopes to get some insights out of this club. Therefore, this concluded why Miss Tia Johnson decided to attend La Salle University and she will be involved in her new community. (Quan Trieu)

2. Write about an experience in which you helped someone bridge the gap from one culture to another. Here is my story. Do you have one like it?

    Soven's story

    I grew up in New York City in the late 1940s and 1950s during the large wave of immigration from Puerto Rico and China. The population in the public schools changed rapidly during those years. To cope with the large influx of nonnative speakers in the school, we were assigned "buddies," that is students who could not speak or write English. We were given fifteen minute breaks during the day to help them. At those times we would answer questions and review our buddy's written work. This was an enormously rewarding experience for both the children who were born in New York and the newcomers. We learned about another culture and language as our new classmates improved their English speaking and writing skills.

3. The Nursing Paper—how would you respond to the first section of this paper that might have been written by a returning adult student in response to this assignment:

Nursing-Career Development Paper Assignment

Select a specific area of nursing in which you would like to practice. The topic needs to be approved by the faculty member. The paper should be word processed and approximately 5–8 pages in length. This does not include title page or bibliography. An interview with a professional nurse is a requirement for the completion of this paper.

Sample Student Paper

A School Nurse

Most childhood memories of school include various objects, people, friends, and overall good times. One very important interaction for most school age children is the role of the school nurse. A school nurse is thought of by most individuals as an older, sweet lady who gives Band-Aids for "boo-boos" and hard candy for sore throats. Unfortunately many individuals are not fully aware of the importance of all the tasks of the school nurse and therefore do not supply he/she with the full credit he/she deserves. The role of the school nurse supplies every student with medical attention, health promotion, educational lessons and guidance, which aid in the child's development. In addition, the school nurse has the responsibility of being an important mediator between a student's family and the surrounding community. The nurse's first responsibility is to insure the safety of the child in all aspects of his/her life. In other words, the career of a school nurse has significant impact in the lives of the children they have reached and therefore should not be overlooked.

Growing up in a family of six children has had a significant impact on my personality and life thus far. Throughout my childhood, I have always enjoyed being around people and helping others, especially children. I feel that I owe most of this attribute to my five siblings, four of them being older. My older brothers and sister were my role models whom I looked up to and yearned to be like.

They along with my parents, were there to nurture, teach and guide me through my path of life. Unfortunately, I have never felt the full satisfaction of being a mentor or had as much impact on a child's life as others have had in mine. Although my younger brother respects my wisdom and guidance. I feel if as I have been just a friend to him.

During childhood I dreamed of being a teacher, but throughout my education my skills and attitude have since changed my attitude to nursing. However, after reflection of my past childhood dreams and viewing of my present skills, I feel that a school nurse is a career that may be right for me.

4. The following paper might have been written in response to an assignment related to the novel, *The Accidental Tourist*, by Anne Tyler. Assume that the paper is written by a good student writer, but that the argument is superficial, since it is rare that good

literature presents easy solutions to difficult problems such as the death of a child. How would you conduct the conference with this student?

Sample Student Paper

The Accidental Tourist: Fathers and Sons

Alexander can be described as a quiet and weak child. Macon and Alexander developed a relationship of bonding after meeting each other. They both helped each other to grow and learn about life and themselves. Macon aided Alexander to grow and provided him with a father he had to admire. Their relationship mirrored a father-son relationship to some extent. Macon undoubtedly showed his support and care for Alexander over time. To begin with, Macon's relationship with Alexander mirrored a father-son relationship in some instances. They began to develop a bond while Macon was living with Muriel. They both impacted each others' lives. For example, Macon taught Alexander how to fix the kitchen sink and encouraged him to be strong and independent, saying, "If he watched he won't know how to fix the one in the bathtub, and I'm going to ask him to manage that without me (240)." Also, after he completed a task, Macon would compliment him by saying encouraging statements, such as, "Wonderful," Very good," and "I believe you have natural talents" (240). Furthermore, he also had Ethan help him to fix pipes and other various household items, while growing up. Macon considered this a bonding experience between him and his son. The same concept applied to Alexander.

Macon ultimately continued to learn about Alexander and grew to care about his feelings and well-being. For example, "So every morning, Macon rose and dressed before Alexander woke. He started fixing breakfast and then roused him (263)." "In the past, he learned, Muriel had often stayed in bed while Alexander woke on his own, got ready for school. sometimes he left the house while she was still asleep. Macon found this shocking (263)." Macon was also concerned with what Alexander would think of him sleeping in the same bed as his mother, he did not want him to get the wrong idea or to assume this was right. This was the reason why Macon rose before Alexander every morning, as courtesy of his feelings.

Once Macon was living with Muriel, Alexander's health began to improve. He was able to be around Edward, whom he loved, without wheezing. It did however make Macon nervous in the beginning for Alexander to be around Edward. "Alexander hugged him and buried his face in Edward's ruff. "Watch it," Macon told him. He had no idea what to do if Alexander started wheezing. But Alexander didn't wheeze. By bedtime he just had a stuffy nose, and he usually had that anyhow (263)." Alexander's bond with Edward resembled the bond that Ethan had with him. Edward became very protective of Alexander and taught him a lot as well. Alexander also became more willing to try specific food items and he could drink milk now without getting sick. He had never drank milk before because it made him throw up, but Macon made him try it and he began to drink it regularly. "Alexander drank milk in the afternoon without complaint (268)." He tried new things and was not afraid of getting sick anymore. He also became more comfortable and trusting of Macon, while complaining less. He found new faith in himself because of Macon.

Macon was also interested in Alexander's education. He would help him with his schoolwork when he came home. "But Macon had the feeling that school never went very well for Alexander. He came out of it with his face more pinched than ever, his glasses thick with fingerprints (268)." Macon felt that his schooling was not equipped and that he would learn better elsewhere. He suggested to Muriel to transfer him into a private school to invest in a better education, wanting him to have the best opportunities available.

Another aspect of the father figure Macon grew into was his concern for his clothes. He took him shopping, "The store he drove to was a Western-wear place where he used to take Ethan. It hadn't changed a bit (297)."

Macon helped Alexander, who was getting taunted, one day after school. When Macon arrived, he said, "Are you all right?" Alexander nodded and got to his feet. "What was that all about?" Macon asked him. Alexander said, "Nothing." but when they started walking again, he slipped his hand into Macon's. Those cool little fingers were so distinct, so particular, and so full of character. Macon tightened his grip and felt a pleasant kind of sorrow sweeping through him. Oh, his life had regained all of its perils. He was forced to worry once again about nuclear war and the future of the planet. He often had the same secret, guilty thought that had come to him after Ethan was born: From this time on I can never be completely happy (292). Macon developed a bond with Alexander that began to resemble the father-son bond he had with Ethan. His bond with Alexander was different than his bond with Ethan, he felt freer until this moment. He felt that now Alexander was in his hands and his responsibility.

Although Macon and Alexander developed a strong bond over time, he would have never been a replacement for Ethan. Macon's relationship with Alexander helped him to overcome the death of his son and helped him to deal with it. Alexander was not A replacement for Ethan because he could never be replaced, but he was a means to an end. They in turn grew and learned from each other. Macon helped Alexander grow into a stronger, more independent individual. Alexander also helped Macon move past Ethan's death and realize there was still a reason for living. He learned from his previous mistakes with Ethan how to be a better father figure to Alexander. When he took Alexander clothes shopping, it brought him to the realization of life going on after death, he thought, "How many times had he done this before? It wasn't even painful. Only disorienting, in a way, to see that everything continued no matter what. The student jeans were still stacked according to waist and inseam. The horsy tiepins were still arrayed behind glass. Ethan was dead and gone but Macon was still holding up shirts and asking, "This one? This one? This one (297)?" On the other hand, sometimes when Macon was helping Alexander with his homework, he would think, "Alexander had managed without him up until now, hadn't he?

There was a peculiar kind of luxury here: Alexander was his own child. Macon felt linked to him in all sorts of complicated ways, but not in that inseparable, inevitable way that he'd been linked to Ethan. He could still draw back from Alexander; he could still give up on him." "The difference was, he realized, that he was not held responsible here. It was a great relief to know that (269)." Although, he felt connected to Alexander in many ways, he did not have an innate responsibility to him, but a chosen one.

5. Compare your own attitudes toward writing to the attitudes of Penny and Mike, the good student writers quoted in the chapter. How are your attitudes similar? How do they differ?

Works Cited

Bartholomae, David. "The Study of Error." *Rhetoric and Composition.* 2nd ed. Ed. Richard Graves. Upper Montclair, NJ: Boynton/Cook Publishers, 1984.

Bizzell, Patricia. "Cognition, Convention, and Certainty, What We Need to Know about Writing." *Academic Discourse and Critical Consciousness.* Pittsburgh, PA: University of Pittsburgh Press, 1992.

Bizzell, Patricia, Bruce Hertzberg and Nedra Reynolds. *The Bedford Bibliography for Writing Teachers.* 5th ed. Boston: Bedford/St. Martins, 2000.

Cech, Maureen and Erin McCarthy. "ESL Students and Writing." Paper Written for English 360, Writing and the University, Philadelphia, La Salle University, 2003.

Horn, Susan. "Fostering Spontaneous Dialect Shift in the Writing of African–American Students." *Dynamics of the Writing Conference: Social and Cognitive Interaction.* Ed. Thomas Lynn and Mary King. Urbana, IL: NCTE, 1993.

Hurlow, Marcia. "Experts with Life, Novices with Writing." *Dynamics of the Writing Conference: Social and Cognitive Interaction.* Ed. Thomas Lynn and Mary King. Urbana, IL: NCTE, 1993.

Kennedy, Mary Lynch. Ed. *Theorizing Composition.* Westport, CT: Greenwood Press, 1998.

Lunsford, Andrea. "The Content of Basic Writers' Essays." *Conference on College Composition and Communication* 31 (October 1980): 278–290.

Neman, Beth. *Teaching Students to Write.* Columbus, OH: Charles E. Merrill Publishing Co., 1980.

Ryan, Leigh. *The Bedford Guide for Writing Tutors.* 2nd ed. Boston: Bedford Books, 1998.

Shaughnessy, Mina P. *Errors and Expectations: A Guide for Teachers of Basic Writing.* New York: Oxford University Press, 1977.

Soven, Margot. "Designing Writing Assignments: Some New Considerations." *Kansas English* (Fall, 1990): 10–19.

Soven, Margot. *Teaching Writing in Middle and Secondary Schools: Research, Theory and Practice.* Needham Heights, MA: Allyn and Bacon, 1999.

Sternglass, Marilyn S. *Time to Know Them: A Longitudinal Study of Writing and Learning at the College Level.* Mahwah, NJ: Lawrence Erlbaum Associates, 1997.

For Further Reading

Cosgrove, Cornelius. " 'Conferencing for the Learning Disabled': How We Might Help." *Dynamics of the Writing Conference: Social and Cognitive Interaction.* Ed. Thomas Flynn and Mary King. Urbana, IL: NCTE, 1993.

Fishman, Stephen M. and Lucille McCarthy. *Whose Goals Whose Aspirations.* Logan, UT: Utah State University Press, 2002.

Franke, Thomas L. "Dyslexia and the College English Teacher." *Teaching English in the Two Year College* 13 (1986): 171–177.

Hirvela, A. "Teaching Immigrant Students in the College Writing Class." *Attending to the Margins: Writing, Research, and Teaching on the Front Lines.* Ed. M. H. Kells and V. Balester. Portsmouth, NH: Boynton/Cook Heinemann, 1999.

Kleinmann, Susan and G. Douglass Meyers. "Senior Citizens and Junior Writers: A Center for Exchange." *Writing Center Journal* 2:1 (1982): 57–60.

7

Teacher Expectations, Writing Assignments, and Peer Tutoring: What's the Connection?

Father Beebe's main concern for his class' first paper were: read-ability, a clear thesis or a main point, and evidence that the students conducted a good amount of research about their topic. He realizes that for many students this is their first experience writing a research paper in college. Many students in the class had not written a paper of this length in high school and were unfamiliar with how to research and cite multiple sources.

—Mary Therese Motley, Writing Tutor, Religion

One thing that I learned between my first and second round of tutoring sessions was just how far off base I was in some of the comments I made on student papers. I was not wrong in the comments I made (or at least I hope I wasn't!), but many of the suggestions I made were not important to the students. My second round of meetings with Dr. Allen revealed to me that her expectations were different than my lofty hopes. Because I was aware only of the information on the assignment sheet and had never met Dr. Allen, I did not realize my expectations were off base.

—Tom McAllister, Writing Tutor, Literature

Through discussion with Mrs. Ryan, I learned that the most important rhetorical elements for her are organization and a consistent point of view, which is especially crucial in the Educational Autobiography. Many students in my conferences, plagued by some of the conventions of academic writing, were hesitant to use the first person. The point of view issue became the most time consuming part of the conferences.

—Stacey Smith, Writing Tutor, Education

Theresa, Tom, and Stacey[1] discovered for themselves that teacher expectations are indeed a "powerful third force in tutoring sessions." In an essay with that title, Belinda Droll argues that peer tutors need to be trained to recognize the rhetorical elements a teacher "emphasizes and rewards" (2). She challenges earlier writing center dogma that emphasized the value of the peer tutor as an independent reader representing an audience other than the instructor. The rationale for the tutor's involvement is that the tutee benefits from having their papers read by two different audiences. Droll explains that although she agrees that the purpose of the writing center is not to "cater to teacher's emphases, but serve the broader purpose of educating students about writing" she takes "[...] the practical position that teacher's expectations are a reality student writers confront daily. Thus as one aspect of tutoring we should help students improve the rhetorical elements of their writing their professors most value" (2).

Droll is right. Writing tutors feel most comfortable when they are aware of teacher expectations. Nevertheless, all writing tutors should make sure that students understand that tutors are not teacher clones. (This point came up in earlier chapters.) Even if they wanted to be teacher stand-ins they couldn't be because, when it comes to grading papers, instructors often apply different criteria than those they originally stated in the assignment. As a peer tutor you cannot predict all the variables that affect students' grades. Sometimes all it takes is one very good paper to influence the instructor's approach to grading the others, sorry to say! But, as the writing tutors' comments which begin this chapter indicate, we cannot ignore the fact that the teacher is present at every tutoring session. Most students are interested in receiving a good grade and want to please their instructor. They see you as the teacher's messenger, if not the teacher's clone, and it is your responsibility, using whatever clues you have, to explain the instructor's expectations as part of the tutoring process.

---

[1]All tutors and instructors quoted in this chapter are from La Salle University.

In this chapter we consider five issues related to teacher expectations:

1. To what degree are teachers' expectations influenced by writing in their disciplines?
2. What are the teachers' criteria for an "A" paper?
3. How does the writing tutor learn about the teacher's expectations?
4. What happens when the tutor thinks that the writing assignment is a poor one?
5. How does the peer tutor balance the two roles—responding as a peer, and responding as a "faculty messenger?"

Teacher's Expectations and Writing in the Disciplines

The first question in the list has been and still is the subject of much debate and research. In the early days of the WAC movement many composition theorists believed that writing assignments are strongly influenced by professional writing in each discipline. They concluded that in contrast composition instructors taught a generic kind of writing which was not related to the kinds of writing assignments in other courses. Theorists felt that students were like "strangers in strange lands" (Maimon). Their task was to learn the languages spoken in these "foreign countries" and the other conventions, such as the preferred format of written documents. For example, sociologists favor an objective writing style and write research reports which follow a specific format: an introduction which includes a hypothesis, followed by a section on methodology and a description of the research. The report culminates with findings and a conclusion. It was assumed that assignments in sociology courses reflect this format, and the format in turn reflects the ways sociologists collect information and analyze it. In literature courses, instructors expect students to use specific punctuation and citation conventions as well as to observe "rules" for including quotations from original sources. For example, I distribute the following list of common errors in literature papers to my students as well as to the writing tutors:

- Citing titles incorrectly
- Omitting lead-ins to quotations
- Inserting quotations without sufficient explanation
- Writing about literature in the past tense
- Omitting citations when summarizing or paraphrasing.

There is no question that teacher expectations are related to conventions of writing in their fields, perhaps more so in advanced courses, but in other courses as well. This conclusion grows naturally from the social constructionist theories discussed in Chapter 1. As Bruffee says in his bibliographic essay on social constructionism, "Social construction understands reality, knowledge, thought, facts, texts, selves, and so on as community generated and community maintained linguistic entities—or more broadly speaking, symbolic entities—that define or 'constitute' the communities that generate them" (774). Each discipline is a community. It would seem obvious that instructors introducing students to their disciplines would use writing assignments to teach the patterns of thinking and the discourse conventions which reflect those patterns. Here is what Stacy, the tutor quoted above, says about writing in different disciplines:

> Often the two goals are compatible, e.g. to teach students about writing and to understand the teacher's expectations, since these expectations often reflect the conventions of their disciplines. By learning to write for Professor X in Psychology, the student often learns the rhetorical elements that most professors of psychology value. When we talk about things like writing introductions, you assume that writing in one discipline improves writing in another discipline. However, they seem at times to work against one another. I see this in my own experience as a result of my dual major. My writing style in Political Science has grown completely separate from my writing style in English.

If you are tutoring in a field that is new to you, you should try to become familiar with the rudiments of the format, style, and documentation conventions of that field. For example, many tutors at La Salle are majors in the humanities. If they are assigned to courses in the School of Nursing, they sometimes erroneously suggest that students eliminate headings and replace the headings with transitional sentences, a convention typical in humanities courses. Instructors will assume that a writing tutor is familiar with discipline-related conventions, such as the APA style of documentation. Instructors in our School of Nursing are especially concerned about their students learning APA. They recently suggested to me that we limit some freshman composition sections to nursing majors to insure that they learn APA documentation.

However, there is another point of view. In "Writing Across the Curriculum: The Vantage of the Liberal Arts," Hedley and Parker claim that especially at colleges with a strong liberal arts curriculum, the similarities between writing assignments in different disciplines are greater than the differences. They challenge the view that "learning to speak the language of particular disciplines is what undergraduate education is all about," except perhaps in advanced courses in major research universities (24). They believe that the goal of most writing assignments is to help students become more reflective thinkers. They say that

> As teachers we discovered that at a certain level we were trying to teach our students similar things: not at the level of the objects themselves, and not in terms of the vocabulary and conventions of scholarly discourse concerning those objects, but at the level on which a process of inquiry yields an interpretive argument, where we help students learn the difference between an argument and a list of examples. (26)

Jennifer Fiolo, a writing tutor at La Salle, makes a similar observation about the writing assignments in a course in religion. Jennifer says that the assignments encourage students not only to "gain insight into the subject, but also to master the skills needed in college writing: critical reading and interpretation" (5).

If this is the case, then writing in freshman composition is good preparation for writing in other courses. Richard Larson's goals for his freshman composition courses are similar to the goals that Hedley and Parker claim are the goals for writing in many courses. He says that in all of his writing courses:

> I work to help students understand what it means to have and express an idea. To have and express an idea includes for me, finding that idea, evaluating it (deciding whether it is worth placing before a reader), putting it into words, explaining it, illustrating it (if it admits of illustration), supporting it, defending it against differing views—in short earning the reader's respect for the idea as developed. (Straub 405–406)

Hedley, Parker, and Larson are describing patterns of thought and language shared by the university as a community, not just by those teachers in a specific discipline.

In research projects conducted by writing tutors at La Salle University, the tutors also found similar kinds of assignments in introductory and intermediate courses, independent of discipline, for example the essay which connects personal experience to the subject matter in the course.

At La Salle we have developed criteria checklists for the kinds of writing assignments typical of many introductory and intermediate courses, using James Kinneavy's rhetorical theories (Soven *Write to Learn* [...] For more information about Kinneavy's theories, read his book *Writing in the Liberal Arts Tradition*.)

Although the criteria we developed at La Salle should not be used slavishly in every situation, you may find them useful especially when the instructor did not include criteria for evaluating the papers in his or her assignment. For example, this is the "Personal Essay Checklist":

The Personal Essay Checklist

1. Does the essay enlighten the reader through an interpretation of self, the self in relation to others, or the self in relation to the world?
2. Is there sufficient description of events and people?
3. Does the essay convey the author's mood or feelings?
4. Has the author responded to all of the questions in the assignment?
5. Is the style personal? (Usually includes the personal pronoun "I," descriptive adjectives, and conversational language.)
6. Are mechanics correct? (Soven 32)

There are many variations on the personal essay assignment. Often these assignments are related to an expanded definition of expressivism found in recent composition theory—namely that achieving self-awareness should lead to social concern. Gradin's *Renouncing Rhetorics* is one of the texts cited as politicizing expressivism (121).

For example, in the core courses in science, students often write essays, not lab reports, about the relationship between science and society. Professor William Price, who teaches chemistry at La Salle, sums up the difference between the writing in core courses in science and the writing in science courses in the major when he says, "In core courses students write about science; in advanced courses, students are taught to write like a scientist." The assignment below was given in a course in Consumer Chemistry, a course students take to meet the science requirements in La Salle's core. Which criteria in the Personal Essay Checklist are related to the assignment? Which criteria are not applicable?

Assignment: The Scientific Discovery that has had the Greatest Effect on My Life

We will discuss many scientific discoveries during the semester. What discovery has affected you the most How? Why? What has been its greatest impact?

Format: Each paper should be three pages in length. References should be properly documented.

Grades: The paper will be graded on Clarity: "Did you focus on one issue? Are the points about the issue made coherently? Do you discuss them Sufficiently?"

Accuracy: Are you using terminology correctly? Are facts correct? Are mechanics correct?

The next assignment comes from a core course in Psychology, "Personality Dynamics and Adjustment." Which criteria in the Personal Essay Checklist are related to the assignment? Which criteria are not applicable?

Select an aspect of your personal life that you would like to understand more fully and that you want to change for the better. You are free to select any aspect of your life that you wish. Describe your thinking, feelings, decisions, and behavior as they relate specifically to the aspect of your personal life you chose to understand more fully. Some examples include the way you study, your relationships with someone: a special friend, parents, a brother or sister, etc. There is no prescribed length for the paper. You might think in terms of four or five double-spaced pages. (Soven 36)

Short essays that require analysis and argumentation are also typical in introductory courses. Some essays require students to support their ideas with personal experience; others require them to use written texts as evidence. Marc Moreau (Philosophy) assigns two short papers to his freshman class, the first one a persuasive argument, and the second a critical analysis. He wants students to learn and develop the skills of persuasion and critical assessment.

Assignment 1: Your goal is to persuade reasonable readers that the position you develop on one of the questions we have discussed is a sensible one. So, whenever you make claims that are open to challenge, your task is to back them up with good reasons.

Assignment 2: Write a critical assessment of the following statement. "Human beings are motivated exclusively by self-interest and they differ from one another, only in their choice of means [. . .]" You should carefully examine its individual claims for potential weaknesses. Explain why you agree or disagree and consider objections and defend them.

To analyze a paper supporting or refuting a claim, I have developed an "Argument" Checklist similar to the Personal Essay Checklist just discussed.

The Argument Checklist

1. Does the introduction include the claim to be argued and definition of key terms?
2. Does the proof of the argument include a clear statement of the supporting claims and sufficient evidence?
3. Does the refutation include a statement of the opposing arguments and evidence to support their refutation?
4. Does the conclusion include a summary of the supporting claims and an emphasis on the importance of the subject?
5. Is the style for the most part objective?
6. Are mechanics correct? (Soven 64)

Try to apply the La Salle Argument Checklist to an essay, which could have been written for another assignment in Dr. Moreau's course, shown in Exercise 1 at the end of the chapter.

What are the Instructor's Criteria for an "A" Paper?

Asking this question seems to defy traditional writing tutor dogma. Although writing tutors are advised to avoid focusing on how the teacher will grade the paper, understanding the instructor's criteria for an "A" paper helps them set priorities with the tutee. You can discuss your understanding of the grading criteria the teacher uses with your tutees without violating the "I can't predict what the grade will be on this paper" rule. Understanding an instructor's grading system can also prevent embarrassment. Writing tutor Steve Martin says, "Ultimately the students were concerned about her [the Professor's] expectations, and I was much more helpful when I understood what she wanted." Steve goes on to say that the first time he met with the student from Dr. Allen's class, he focused heavily on what I have been describing as higher-order concerns: focus, organization, and development. He adds, "Even when Dr. Allen warned me that one girl had problems with usage, I missed the hint. The student left her meeting with me praising her paper. I was upset when I learned that she had received a C+ on the paper. I began all of my second round conferences with two questions: Is there anything your teacher commented on in your last paper, that you want to improve or that you do not understand?' " Steve learned to remain alert to the instructor's expectations.

How Does the Writing Tutor Learn About Instructor's Expectations?

Information about instructors' grading practices is often not easy to come by, especially if you are tutoring in a writing center where you are working with students from many classes. You may get this information through the grapevine. As you know, some instructors develop reputations for "grading hard" and others for distributing "A"s liberally. However, there are more systematic ways to learn about teacher's grading policies. For example, the writing center director, with the aid of the writing tutors, can survey the faculty via email. Ask the faculty to describe their grading criteria. With the authorization of your writing center director, you might interview faculty who typically send their students to the writing center. The director of the center can also invite faculty to discuss their grading criteria during informal meetings.

If you are lucky the assignment instructions will include criteria for grading (not all teachers do this), but even the instructors who include general evaluation criteria in their assignments will rarely describe the "A"paper, the "B" paper, and so on. (See Moreau's assignment, grading criteria in Exercise 1.)

As you know from your experience as a student, instructors have different standards when it comes to grades. Even instructors in the same department often disagree. Some place more emphasis on the quality of the ideas or information in the paper, others on style (using criteria similar to those in the Personal Essay Checklist), and still others on correct mechanics. There are instructors (notably in English Departments) who want the "A" paper to be *inventive*, using Claire Busse's phrase. She will not give the "A" grade if the paper simply "regurgitates class notes." She says that the "A" paper, regardless of the level of the course, "[...] should surprise me. It should reflect a process of thought and discovery, though it doesn't necessarily need to break new ground. If it has some 'brilliance' to it, then I will overlook some grammatical flaws." In contrast, Vincent Kling, also in the English Department at La Salle, makes a distinction between criteria for evaluating papers in introductory versus advanced courses. It is only in advanced courses that Professor Kling expects the "A" paper to include an "original point or impression."

In many courses students receive an "A" for competency rather than originality. For example, in the Religion Department, Father David Beebe, quoted earlier in the chapter, emphasizes the quality of the students' research when he arrives at a grade. He believes that a major objective for writing in core courses is to teach students how to do research. He expects a certain number of errors on the sentence level and does not penalize students for them. Sr. Roseanne McDougall, another instructor in the Religion Department, stresses structure.

In the Philosophy Department, Marc Moreau wants students to "take a stand" in their papers. For him the "A" paper must include a good argument that demonstrates that the student has recognized possible objections to his argument and refutes them. For Moreau, the "B" paper will use weaker arguments than the "A" paper.

My own description of an "A" paper includes the provision that it must be "inviting to read," by which I mean that it is coherent, the relationships between the ideas explicit, and the sentences rhetorically effective. For example, in a literature class where the assignment topics are in the form of questions, I use the following grading scale:

An "A" paper answers the questions in a comprehensive manner. It shows good reasoning and evidence. The paper demonstrates a strong sense of coherence, sentence structure is fluent and, for the most part, free from errors in usage, punctuation, and spelling.

A "B" paper is less comprehensive in its treatment of the question. It lacks the sense of coherence that characterizes the "A" paper, but a plan of organization is obvious. It may also lack the fluency of sentence structure that characterizes the "A" paper, but will be for the most part free from errors in usage, punctuation, and spelling.

A "C" paper is often characterized by simplicity of thought. The writing seems thin because ideas are not sufficiently developed, although the student has attempted to answer the question. The plan for organization may be less obvious than in the "B" paper, and fluency of sentence structure will most likely be absent. The "C" paper may have more errors in usage, punctuation, and spelling than the "B" paper.

I don't bother describing the "D" and "F" papers. Instead, if a paper is not in the "C" range, I refuse to grade it until the student revises it. The students you tutor are often afraid to ask their teacher about grading criteria. I can only guess at the reasons for their reluctance; perhaps they think that the instructor will think that their interest in the course is confined to the grade. You can act as the go-between. Ideally, teacher and tutor should be working together. Once again, we turn to Bruffee's notion of the tutor as translator; you can help students interpret their instructors' grading criteria.

What Happens When the Assignment is Unclear or Poorly Designed?

I'm sure you are experts on the subject of poor assignments. Having completed dozens of assignments yourself, you know a good one when you see it, but you also have been dealt your share of vague, or even worse, impossible assignments. A poor assignment is one of the most frustrating problems you will encounter as a writing tutor.

For example, sometimes the page limit will be unrealistic given what the student is asked to accomplish in the assignment. A writing tutor at La Salle, Tim McManus, had this to say about an assignment:

> The most obvious problem in this round of conferences was in the quality of the papers. They were not as good as the papers in the first round. I felt that contributing to the problem was the very demanding assignment in which students had four pages to discuss four poems—their poetic style, analysis and background material, and then they had to relate each poem to their personal experience. I had a hard time telling them how to cram so much information into so little space. One student gave me a five page paper analyzing just one poem. If she followed the assignment and discussed four poems, she would have handed in a twenty page essay!

Other assignments are poor because they require students to write about unfamiliar subjects. The students do not have sufficient knowledge to do the assignment. Tim once again provides a good description of this problem.

> The assignment asked students to develop two methods that would reduce the influence of money on the media. Because Communication is my major, I know that a logical argument on this subject would take monumental research. Since the articles the students were required to read were not relevant, I found the students' arguments to be illogical and unrealistic. It wasn't their fault. The assignment required them to develop a miracle solution to a problem about which they had no expertise.

There is no magic pill for helping students with a poor assignment. If you are tutoring in a writing center, you may want to ask the director to contact the instructor. If you are a Writing Fellow and assisting students in a single class, be brave and request a meeting with the instructor. Faculty have been known to revise assignments after they become aware of the difficulties students are having completing them. If you are not able to contact the instructor, then suggest to the student he or she check with the instructor after class.

How Does the Tutor Balance the Two Roles: Responding as a Tutor, and Responding as a Faculty Messenger?

Writing tutor Denise Maher says,

> Although I know what the instructor wanted, I had to create my own hierarchy of concerns for each student's paper. Each student seemed to be at a different stage of writing development, and each student had different problems in their papers. I had to tell myself to focus on the biggest problem in the paper, but also to keep in mind the many things important to the teacher. The way I did this was always to refer the student back to the assignment sheet during the tutoring session.

Denise is a good example of a writing tutor who understands that knowing the teacher's expectations is just one part, albeit an important one, of the writing tutor's responsibilities. She must still decide how to conduct the tutoring session in light of the condition of the paper and what she learns about the student, from both the paper, and meeting the student in person if she has that opportunity.

I will end this chapter with a brief set of guidelines which acknowledge the important role that "invisible" instructors play when you tutor writing:

- Expect strong similarities in teachers' expectations for papers in introductory courses. Instructors are concerned about teaching students the basics of academic discourse and assigning writing that connects course content with students' personal lives.
- Don't be afraid of tutoring a student with a paper in a field which is new to you. If you are not familiar with the documentation conventions in the discipline, be sure to locate information about these conventions. Documentation style guides for most disciplines are readily available in composition handbooks and online.
- Become familiar with the format conventions of papers in the field. For example, if the assignment calls for a report, be sure to obtain a copy of a model report in the field in which the assignment is written.
- If you don't have a copy of the assignment, or the instructor did not give the instructions in writing, ask the student about the assignment, but don't assume his version is gospel truth. Students' perceptions are not always accurate. Just recently a student told

me that she was penalized for stating her opinion in a paper, when the teacher had explicitly asked for her opinion. Not so. I learned from the instructor that she required a critique, "supported with evidence." By "evidence" she meant evidence from readings, not from the student's personal views.

- Try to meet with instructors who routinely send their students to the writing center. If you are tutoring in a curriculum-based peer-tutoring program (for example a Writing Fellows program), meetings with the instructor will often be a part of the program. Denise pointed out that the instructor whose class she assisted urged her to "talk to him if problems arose. He was always there to respond to emails if I had any questions." If you meet with the instructor, ask the instructor for a model paper. Some instructors save good papers from previous semesters.

And, finally, keep in mind that there is no such thing as the perfect writing assignment. I know from my own teaching experience that developing good writing assignments is one of the greatest challenges of teaching. Often both in and outside the classroom we must perform tasks that are not described as well as they could be.

Questions for Discussion and Writing

1. Evaluate this essay that could have been written in a philosophy class using Dr. Moreau's criteria.

Writing Assignment

Should we adopt a speech code on our campus? As the term is used here, a speech code is a policy of attaching penalties to abusive speech that stigmatizes groups of individuals in particularly offensive ways. A typical speech code prohibits speech that (1) is directly addressed to particular individuals; (2) contains derogatory references to the race, gender, disability, ethnic identity, or sexual orientation of those individuals; and (3) is inherently likely to create an intimidating, hostile, or demeaning environment for those individuals. If adopted here, the prohibition could be applied to all members of the La Salle community, including faculty, staff, and students; and persons found in violation of the speech code could be subject to various forms of discipline, possibly including discharge for an employee and expulsion for a student. To investigate and enforce complaints raised against members of the community, a special review board (composed perhaps of faculty, staff, and students) would have to be created. And to protect the rights of all parties, due process would have to be established; e.g., alleged violators must be given an opportunity to respond to the complaints, and where possible, neutral witnesses must be interviewed.

Your assignment is this: Answer my opening question and give a reasoned defense of your answer. If you think that a speech code of some sort is advisable but have misgivings about elements of the "typical" code outlined in the preceding paragraph, you are at liberty to introduce any modifications you deem appropriate–provided that you justify those modifications. Do not, however, lose sight of the central question, "Should we adopt a speech code on our campus?" Your main task is to persuade your reader that the answer you have given to this moral question is a reasonable one.

Let me remind you that any instance of plagiarism—the act of passing off another's work as your own—will earn an automatic "F" on the assignment. For this assignment, you are not required to use secondary sources; but if you do, you must cite your sources at the end of your paper and at every point of use. (Any standard method of citation is acceptable.) Quotations from our text may be cited by page numbers alone.

The grading will be based both on the quality of your ideas and on the quality of your writing. The checklist that follows is meant to indicate the range of considerations that will enter my evaluation of your paper.

Spelling and Vocabulary: Are your words spelled correctly? Is your word choice appropriate? Is it precise? (When in doubt consult a dictionary.) Grammar: Are your sentences complete? Do your verbs agree with their subjects? Do your pronouns agree with their antecedents? Are your tenses consistent? Have you made correct use of commas, semi-colons, colons, apostrophes, and quotation marks? (Consult a grammar book.)

Style: Are your sentences wordy? Have you used twenty-five words where five would do? Are your sentences awkward?

Composition: Is your essay a unified and orderly whole? Is it built around a clearly identified thesis? Have you indicated how each part of your paper contributes to its central project? (Note: Vis-À-vis the present assignment, your thesis is your answer to my opening question, and your project is to defend this answer as a reasonable one. So you can enhance the organizational clarity of your paper by including a clear statement of your thesis in your introduction. If you do not at the outset identify the thesis you intend to support, your readers will lack the information they need in order to appreciate the purpose and significance of the points you make along the way.) Are the transitions from paragraph to paragraph coherent? (Have you included transitional comments that can help your reader follow the turns in your thought?) Is each paragraph well focused around a topic sentence?

The clarity, consistency, and significance of the points you make: Does your paper contain statements that are obscure or ambiguous? Do you contradict yourself? Do you make trite observations?

The rigor, thoroughness, and inventiveness of your arguments: Is your reasoning sound? Does it contain fallacies? Do your arguments rest on unsubstantiated claims or on unexamined assumptions? Have you neglected information that could put your inferences into jeopardy? In defending your thesis have you made only the most obvious points? Or have you managed your case with some resourcefulness and imagination?

Your alertness to potential objections and your appreciation of alternative viewpoints: Have you addressed objections that a critic would be likely to raise? Have you done so in a way that effectively neutralizes them? Have you done justice to the strengths and insights of perspectives that compete with your own?

Your mastery of relevant concepts: Have you accurately presented the ideas contained in your sources? Have you correctly applied them?

The aptness and richness of any analogies or illustrations you may use: Where they are needed to clarify or develop a point you're trying to make, have you made use of suitable analogies or illustrations? Do your analogies or illustrations genuinely enhance your direct statements? Or do they instead mislead-say, 'by introducing themes that are irrelevant or even antagonistic to your project?'

Sample Student Essay

It is the first day of school and unlike previous years at La Salle a Code of Ethics Booklet is given to each returning student as well as freshmen students, which must be reviewed, signed and dated to assure that everyone is familiar with and understand the new code of ethics. This code was established by the faculty, staff and students of La Salle to allow one to become familiar with the code of ethics in the work force and the importance of conduct during community service. If for any reason the student, staff or faculty members fail to sign and date the booklet stating they understand the codes, they will not be allowed on La Salle's property.

I believe La Salle University should adopt a speech code on campus. La Salle is a Christian University and is known worldwide for its catholic beliefs. Although La Salle's staff, faculty and students many not directly practice Catholicism, or the universities' Christian practices are not enforced on them, I believe all faculty and students should respect the campus' grounds and facilities.

Using derogatory or abusive language is not good morals and should not be tolerated. La Salle's name and reputation when mentioned is above all and people have respect for the university. Parents and guardians trust sending their children to a private university and do not mind spending the extra money. I believe if the conduct code was enforced it would not only teach faculty vs. faculty and faculty vs. students to respect one another, but it will also have an affect on students respecting their fellow classmates.

Many students leave home with the impression or thought of getting out of their parents' home and becoming free. They no longer feel they are confined to guardianship or parental guidance, and believe they can do on campus all the things that were not tolerated at home. Some leave campus with a college degree and no morals.

College is not a play thing. It is designed to make a person well rounded and able to adapt in the world. The' advantages of a Christian university, *is* one that will make one well rounded and not only to help one adapt in the real world, but to teach one respect for their fellow brethren.

Attending a Christian university should be so vital and so important that one should be highly reprimanded for disrespecting any member of the facility. Whether the crime is fighting, name calling, rape, theft [...] anything that is morally wrong according to the Christian code of ethics.

I believe that a disciplinary committee of both faculty and students should be formed along with a code of ethics guideline. Anyone in violation of any of the codes would have to go through this committee. There would also be a supreme committee which would decide one's penalty if an appeal was made. If there is question about whether the party is guilty or innocent there would also be a jury formed. After a fair trial one would be sentenced. There punishment could be anything from suspension, being reprimanded, receiving a fine or penalty, to perform community services or even a more severe punishment as being expelled from the University.

Although this may seem like a hard task that one must go through these rules must be enforced to assure that we do not lose students or faculty because of rudeness or misconduct. The world as well as the workforce are looking for well-groomed individuals who are upright and honest in character. With a code of ethics being enforced, La Salle's students can walk up tall and be moral, honest abiding citizens. With this training La Sale's alumni can also train the children and be a positive example to society.

La Salle also believes in their students being involved in community services and students should be taught to carry themselves in a way that would reflect a positive attitude toward the school. No conduct should be allowed that would cause the character any La Salle staff, student or faculty to be questioned.

2. Read the instructor's assignment and evaluation criteria. Using his or her criteria, evaluate this paper which might have been written in response to the assignment.

Length—approximately 2–3 typed pages (double-spaced)
Assignment—Choose one of the following:

A. An analysis of one of the poems by Keats listed below in which you focus on one or two elements that Keats uses to reveal the poem's meaning.
B. An analysis of one stylistic device or motif that appears in two or more of Keats' poems, explaining how Keats uses this device or motif.

For A or B, you can choose from the following poems (for B you can choose also one poem from those studied in class):

" 'I stood tip-toe upon a little hill [. . .]: *3–10*
" 'How many bards gild the lapses of time! [. . .]: *39–40*
"On the Grasshopper and Cricket": *45*
"Sleep and Poetry": *47–58*
"Lamia": *187–207*
"Isabella; or The Pot of Basil": *208–223*
"Ode to Psyche": *240–242*
"Fancy": *242–244*
"Ode on Melancholy": *250–251*
"To Lord Byron": *282*
"On sitting down to read 'King Lear' once again": *297*
"Lines on seeing a Lock of Milton's Hair": *299–300*
"To Sleep": *346*
"Ode on Indolence": *358–360*

NOTE—KEEP IN MIND THE FOLLOWING:

- You need to read the poem several times and think about what Keats is doing and why.
- You want to give your paper a title that relates to your thesis (for example Imagery in Keats' Poem).
- You want to support your thesis as you would argue with specific examples from the text of the poem(s) and not as an unsupported expression of likes and dislikes—nor as merely plot summary.
- You want to *either paraphrase or quote the text to* support your point, but whatever you do, you do want to use MLA parenthetical documentation.
- If you do use any outside critical support, you do want to supply a "Works Cited" page (also in MLA format).
- As with all your writing, you want to check for the correct grammar, punctuation, and mechanics. Sentence structure errors (run-ons, fragments, or comma splices) particularly will lower your grade. Therefore, please proofread carefully.

Sample Essay on Keats' Poem, "The Grasshopper and the Cricket"

The poem On the Grasshopper and Cricket,' by John Keats is a fine example of Keats' fondness of nature and how he uses it in his poems to convey meaning. In this particular poem, he uses both the grasshopper and the cricket to show how "the poetry of earth is never dead -in other words, Keats believes that nature never stops and has no limits. He illustrates this thesis by using two different seasons as well as two different insects.

The first element to be discussed is that of the grasshopper. The grasshopper's portion of the poem is set on what seems to be a hot summerday. We see this when he writes, "When all the birds are faint with the hot sun, And hide in cooling trees [. . .]" Amidst the hot sun he hears a voice that moves about the brush. This is the voice of the grasshopper., He writes, "That is the Grasshopper's – he takes the lead in summer luxury, he has never done With his delights; for when tired out with fun, He rests at ease beneath some pleasant weed". Here Keats talks about the grasshopper and how he feels that it sings it song all day and when it gets tired it just rests under a leaf or plant. It seems as though he wishes he were able to lead the same carefree life as the grasshopper. This is a theme that occurs in many of Keats' poems such as "Ode to a Nightingale."

The second element that Keats uses in the poem is that of the cricket. At the start of the cricket's verse, he uses a-similar statement to open it as he did the grasshopper's He writes, "The poetry of earth is ceasing never" I believe he put this here just to keep the theme of the poem fresh in reader's minds. The season has changed from a hot summer day to a cold winter evening. We see this in "On a lone winter evening, when the frost Has wrought a silence, All of the sounds of nature that were present in the summer have gone, including that of the, grasshoppers." But there is a new sound to take the place of it. He writes, "from the stove there shrills The Cricket's song, in warmth increasing ever." This illustrates Keats' belief that nature is never ceasing; it is alive on both the hottest of days and the coldest. The grasshopper sings its song in the summer while the cricket does likewise in the winter.

The Grasshopper's among some grassy hill.' thinks here he is saying that as the cricket sings his song he can faintly hear the grasshoppers in the distance. Maybe meaning that as winter comes near its end, the grasshopper begins to sing its song once more, showing the infinite cycle that nature goes through.

The third element he uses is the use of the seasons. He uses summer and winter, two opposite seasons, to show how nature changes but at the same times stays the same. The grasshopper was his focus in the summer while the cricket was the focus in the winter. He uses them to show how they both take each other's place in nature as seasons change. The cricket picks up the song where the grasshopper leaves o4and vice versa. Nature never dies; it just comes in different forms at different times. This is what he means when he says, "The poetry of earth is never dead,"

In conclusion, Keats uses nature, specifically the grasshopper, the cricket, and the. seasons to illustrate how nature continues on forever. His use of nature imagery helps him to convey his meaning and does so very well. Along with this, and many of his other poems, Keats shows interest and love of nature and writes about it elegantly.

Works Cited

Bruffee, Kenneth A. "Social Construction, Language and the Authority of Knowledge: A Bibliographical Essay." *College English* 48 (1986): 773–790.

Droll, Belinda. "Teacher Expectations: A Powerful Third Force in Tutoring Sessions." *Writing Lab Newsletter*, May, 1993. 1–5.

Fiolo, Jennifer. Final Project in *Writing and the University*, La Salle University, 2003.

Gradin, Sherrie. *Romanticizing Rhetorics: Social Expressivist Perspectives on the Teaching of Writing*. Portsmouth, NH: Boynton/Cook, 1995.

Hedley, Jane and Jo Ellen Parker. "Writing Across the Curriculum: The Vantage of the Liberal Arts." *ADE Bulletin* 98 (1991): 23–28.

Kinneavy, James L., Neil Nakadate, and William J. McLeary. *Writing in the Liberal Arts Tradition*. 2nd ed. New York: Harper and Row, 1990.

Larson, Richard. "A Statement of 'Philosophy' About Teaching Writing." *Twelve Readers Reading: Responding to Student Writing*. Ed. Richard Straub and Ron Lunsford. Cresskill, N.V: Hampton Press, Inc., 1995. 405–406.

Maimon, Elaine. "Talking to Strangers." *College Composition and Communication* 30 (1979): 364–369.

Maimon, Elaine. "Maps and Genres: Exploring Connections in the Arts and Sciences." *Composition and Literature: Bridging the Gap*. Ed. Winifred Horner. Chicago, IL: University of Chicago Press, 1983.

Soven, Margot. *Write to Learn: A Guide to Writing Across the Curriculum*. Cincinatti, OH: South-Western College Publishing, 1996.

For Further Reading

Bazerman, Charles and David R. Russell. *Landmark Essays on Writing Across the Curriculum*. Davis, CA: Hermagoras Press, 1994.

Behrens, Laurence and Leonard Rosen. *Writing and Reading Across the Curriculum*. 8th ed. New York: Longman Press, 2003.

Herrington, Anne and Charles Moran. Ed. *Writing, Teaching, and Learning in the Disciplines*. New York, MLA: 1992.

Hunt, Doug. *Misunderstanding the Assignment*. Portsmouth, NH: Boynton-Cook, 2002.

8

Tutoring Online: An Option—But Is It a Good One?

Dear tutor, Can I email my draft to you tonight? I can have it to you by 3am. By the way, it's due for my 9:00 class. Please advise. Thanks much!

The electronic world beckons. How many of your friends would prefer to live "online" except for the weekend fraternity party or to answer their cell phones! At times it seems that college "off line" is a thing of the past. When a librarian recommends checking the catalog for a book on some subject, her suggestion is often met with a blank stare. Perhaps the student thinks:

> Book? Does that mean that I need to go to the second or third floor, find the book, remove it from the shelf, return to the first floor and check it out? Hm—sounds pretty exhausting. Actually, I wasn't even planning to leave my room to do this paper, but unfortunately I can't find my subject on Google!

Sound familiar? In a recent study conducted by writing tutors at La Salle, "Students' Use of Online Resources," the tutors reported that 100 percent of the students in the study named a general search engine (for example Google or Yahoo) as the starting point for their research (Davis, DeMedio, Greathouse).

Ironically, your instructors and librarians are contributing to "computer psychosis." You can find your syllabi and writing assignments online, maybe even the instructor's lectures, as well as much of the material you need for your research papers. As you know, you can use the library from the comfort of your dorm room. Are the classroom and the library becoming obsolete? Is the writing center next?

I don't think so. Your teachers want you to come to class. As I tell my students, although I can't possibly give an exam that measures the value of class discussion, I believe that personal contact with them is essential for a successful course. The librarians, too, are there to help you. A trip to the library can reduce the time you waste scrolling through useless websites. Most peer tutors, writing program administrators, and instructors agree that the benefits of face-to-face, one-on-one personal meetings are greater than written comments alone or online tutoring. Marjorie Allen, a professor in the English Department at La Salle, says, "I can't be sure that the student understands my comments unless she is sitting in front of me. I keep asking questions and explaining comments until I think that the student has enough and the right information to revise." Research supports the effectiveness of one-on-one conferencing—recall the discussion in Chapter 3 about conferences. Reigstad and McAndrew say "[. . .] face to face tutoring is the preferred method of peer tutoring, not only because it keeps the human elements at maximum but also because all [most] of the research that supports tutoring assumed face to face tutoring, therefore face to face tutoring is the only mode that has fully developed research ground" (12).

Face-to-face tutoring also has theoretical clout. Recall the social constructionist emphasis on the importance of conversation in learning how to write. Conversation also fits the writing as process paradigm. For example, Emily Meyer and Louise Smith, authors of *The Practical Tutor*, emphasize the importance of conversation during the planning phase of writing as a "precursor of ideas" (27). Cooper, Bui, and Riker point out, from a social constructionist, process-oriented point of view of tutoring writing, that "online tutoring stretches the viability of these good principles. One could argue that sending a paper online to a tutor can be similar to dropping off dry cleaning—leave your paper at the center on Monday and pick it up on Tuesday with all errors marked and corrected—a practice abhorred in most writing centers" (92).

However, there is increasing support for online tutoring. McAndrew and Reigstad believe that electronic communication technologies "offer a theoretically sound medium for tutoring" because they expand the "time and space for tutoring, making tutoring available to writers, even if it is in a reduced form, in ways that blend with many people's writing processes and lives" (120). The online conversation has its own conventions, different from, but perhaps not less effective, than the conversation which takes place in face-to-face tutoring. In "Writing Centers and WAC" Joan Mullin shows support for this view when she says that online activities [similar to face-to-face tutoring] change the way students use language and in fact they will have "immense repercussions on discipline specific knowledge making" (191). Mullin implies that online tutoring will affect not only students but their teachers as well. These frequent "conversations" with students may result in a new discourse for conveying the knowledge of their disciplines, which may in fact change the discourse of the discipline itself.

Online tutoring also advances the objectives of individualizing education and understanding the learning process by providing continuous feedback to both the instructor and the student. As Mullin points out, during online tutoring "language is being renegotiated and faculty, students, and the [writing] center are responding to immediate and contextual needs" (191). In addition to theoretical support, there are at least six good reasons (there may be more) for using electronic tutoring as a powerful supplement, if not a replacement for face-to-face tutoring.

- Students *like* using technology. They associate technology with fun—computer games, endless hours of emailing their friends, exchanging jokes, and so on. Even faculty members can be caught playing solitaire online during their office hours!
- Students are experts at communicating online. They belong to the generation that has been using instant messaging since junior high school and assume that information comes via technology.
- Electronic tutoring can be an ice breaker. For some students face-to-face tutoring can be uncomfortable. Some faculty at Temple University say that email "removes issues of gender, age, race, and personality, allowing both parties to focus on tutoring. [Student] feedback [to online tutoring] has been positive" (Valenza). These same students may be motivated to continue to work on their writing in the writing center after their online tutoring experience.
- Electronic tutoring fits the changing university. Teachers are using online chatrooms for discussion outside of class, courses are often taught in computer labs, and courses in computer literacy are required by many colleges and universities. Gillespie and Lerner are on the mark when they say that, as "institutions of higher learning turn increasingly to technology to deliver instruction, the online writing center will become much more the norm, if not the model for how to blend technology and pedagogy" (146).

- An increasing number of studies support the effectiveness of teaching writing online. For example, the University of Pennsylvania recently completed a study comparing the writing of students in composition courses taught online to the writing of students in standard classroom-based writing courses. Both approaches were equally successful (Kuriloff).
- The number of so-called "unconventional students" is growing. Your school probably offers courses in the evenings and on weekends to busy students who cannot come to the writing center during office hours. They may not come to campus at all if they are in a distance learning course. Although it may not be the ideal, in circumstances where students cannot take advantage of one-on-one conferencing, electronic tutoring makes it possible for other students to get help with their writing. At La Salle, we use online tutoring in writing for students at our branch campuses.

Online tutoring advocates believe that "though principles of face-to-face tutoring do not transfer completely to online tutoring, we can still retain a sense of collaboration and humanity in the online forum" (Cooper 92). Online tutoring can become a shared experience if we use certain techniques. In this chapter, I describe various kinds of electronic tutoring, explain how to maximize the benefits of electronic tutoring, and avoid some of the pitfalls associated with this relatively new form of tutoring.

Synchronous and Asynchronous Electronic Tutoring

Become familiar with these two terms. You will meet them again and again in the literature about electronic tutoring. *Asynchronous tutoring* refers to tutoring situations that are not happening in real time. For example, the student sends you a paper as an attachment. You read it some time afterward and return it with comments. Then the student may write back to you after receiving your comments. This is an example of asynchronous tutoring.

Synchronous tutoring occurs when you are in immediate dialogue with the student. Tutor and student simultaneously view the text. The dialogue can be written or verbal (for example a conversation on the telephone) but you are exchanging comments in real time. Asynchronous tutoring seems to be the more popular of the two online modes since it permits both the student and the tutor to work when it's best for them. It's the less complicated of the two, but not necessarily the most effective. As I write this book, there is not enough research on either approach to claim that one is better than the other, but it is clear that the two modes produce different results. For example, Honeycutt found that "when using email (asynchronous conferencing) students made significantly greater reference to documents, their contents and rhetorical contexts than when using synchronous conferencing, whereas students made greater reference to both writing and response tasks using synchronous chats than when using email." Interestingly, when asked which approach was more effective in helping them to revise, students made no distinction between the usefulness of comments in either approach in aiding revision (Honeycutt 26).

If you plan to try electronic tutoring online, the approach you take will depend a great deal on the students you serve. For example, the asynchronous model is probably best when you work with students who are hard to reach. They may be taking evening courses and working during the day. The chances that you can arrange a time when you both are at the computer may be slim. If you are tutoring students who have easy access to a computer, and you work in a writing center with software that permits synchronous chats (email dialogues), then you can also try out synchronous tutoring. For example, Instant Messaging is one type of Internet software that facilitates email dialogue. Another type of software called MUDS or MOOs are also being used for this purpose. Word 2004 has an Online Collaboration Function that permits synchronous conferencing.

What Kind of Feedback Should Students Expect Online?

The impulse to edit the tutee's paper when commenting online is even greater than it is when commenting on a hard copy of the paper. To avoid this pitfall, most experts agree that when commenting online, your focus should be on issues that affect the whole paper rather than on simple sentence-level issues. For this reason electronic tutoring may be less effective than one-on-one conferencing for students with significant sentence level problems, such as ESL students. Many schools have policies similar to the Boston College Online Writing Lab (OWL). Their guidelines describe the kinds of comments students can expect:

In the same way that sending an e-mail differs from face to face conversation, online tutoring differs from in-person tutoring. Rather than comment on the sentence level, your OWL tutor will emphasize broader, more conceptual issues and rhetorical issues. Such comments include affirmation of parts of your writing that work well, questions to consider as you revise, and advice about general ways to for improving your work. Your tutor may also offer you the opportunity to engage in an active dialogue about your writing in progress.

The Boston College Online guidelines include this warning:

> The OWL is not a proofreading or editing service. Any requests for such services will result in your paper being returned to you exactly as it arrived.

Like most online services, the Boston College OWL also reminds students that the tutor will not predict a grade.

Some schools, such as Purdue University, will not offer students an online response to their entire essay. These are the Purdue OWL guidelines:

> We are glad to respond via email to a question or two from anyone who asks, but unfortunately we lack the resources to comment extensively on drafts or papers [. . .] we will offer feedback on specific portions of a paper (such as an introduction, a sample body paragraph or a conclusion) sent as a part of a text-only email message. (2)

What Kinds of Comments Work Best Online?
Front Comments

Barbara Monroe ("Wiring the Writing Center") favors using what she calls a front comment, intertextual comments, and an end comment. The front comment tells the student how to read the comments. For example, the tutor might write, "I have added some comments to your paper. They appear as yellow highlighted words. To view the comments, let your cursor rest on a yellow word and a box will pop up with the comment in it. To delete the comment, right click on the yellow word and select 'delete comment' " (Kastman-Breuch et al.). An opening comment can help you establish a relationship with the student, the same way you would as you begin a writing conference. For example,

> Hi Morton, I'm Lisa, the OWL tutor who will be reading your paper. I've read through your questions and will make some notes within your paper about the intro, the conclusion, the overall structure of your paper, and grammar. I'll also try to include major questions I have as a reader, as I read, so you can

get an idea of how an average reader might react. Look for my notes within the body of your paper set off by asterisks, like this****. (Cooper 93)

Once you get to the end comments and the intertextual comments, be especially careful about avoiding jargon. Ryan Hoffmaster (the La Salle writing tutor introduced earlier in the book) became aware of the importance of being precise. He says, "As I formulated comments to the students, I found it rather challenging to communicate in such a way that I could be sure that they were understanding my intentions."

End Comments

Begin as you would in a writing conference when commenting on a printed copy of the paper by giving your general impression of the paper in an end comment (called a summary comment in Chapter 3). Referring to specific parts of the paper, typically the next step in responding to an essay, is more difficult than when you have the printed copy in hand. However, but there are several techniques you can use for this purpose.

For example, you can use asterisks or bold face or both, if you would like for the kinds of comments you would normally write in the margin. For example,

> Flannery O'Connor writes about women who are dominated by men in many of her stories. **Can you give an example from one of her stories?** a male character whose motives are not good ones often defeats them.

If you are familiar with the "comments" function you can use pop-ups to write comments in the margin. Don't forget to explain to students how to use the pop-up function if you choose it for some of your comments.

In either the end comment or the intertextual comments you can try to promote dialogue, for example, ask questions. Although the student may not return the answer, questions "suggest openness, a give and take between writer and tutor" (Cooper 94). In the absence of facial expressions and body language, questions help to establish the persona of the tutor as a peer rather than a teacher. For example,

> ****You seem to think that all the male characters in Flannery O'Connor's stories are evil. Have you considered the possibility that they are also smarter than the women, and for that reason, they control them? Do the women in her stories seem to take action based on reason or based on bias and prejudice? I'm not sure myself, but I think it may be an interesting question to explore in your paper, if you think so too.****

Sentence Level Comments

Although you shouldn't edit papers, you can still give sentence level advice without falling into the editing trap. Here's an example of a comment about sentence problems:

> I think you should proofread your paper carefully before turning it in. Check for comma errors in compound sentences which require a comment before conjunctions such as "and" or "but." For example, "The boy went to the store, **and** he bought candy" is a compound sentence.

You can also remind students to use the grammar check and spell-check functions. Believe it or not, some students are in too much of a rush to even do that! Another idea: If you are working with a student online you might suggest that he create some work space between sentences or paragraphs to try out some alternative wording. The new sentences can be written in italics to set them off from the text. For example, you might say, "I find that sentence hard to understand. Try another way of saying your idea." We often take this approach during face-to-face conferences.

Low-Tech Electronic Tutoring: The Telephone

When we hear "electronic tutoring" we rarely think about the telephone, but tutors and teachers have been helping students by telephone for years. Long before email, writing centers had telephone hotlines. Although they may have abandoned the formal phone hotline, both instructors and tutors still receive questions about writing by phone. Sometimes the questions are specific, such as "May I read you this sentence to you and ask if I need a comma after 'and'?" If you work in a writing center that still offers telephone hotline service, or you receive an occasional call from a student asking for writing advice, I suggest that you jot down the sentence in question before responding. If the student wants you to comment on a paragraph or a short paper by phone, ask many of the same questions as you would face to face. Find out as much as you can about the assignment and when the paper is due. If the paper isn't due the next day, it may pay to ask the student to email or fax it to you.

Oddly, there may be an educational advantage to discussing an assignment without a printed copy in hand. When students know that you do not have a copy of the paper, they may try harder than they do at conferences to verbalize the problems they have writing the paper, thereby participating more actively in solving these problems than do the students you meet face to face (McAndrew and Reigstad 121).

Many writing centers now offer an online "hotline" service. For example, at Temple University the writing center staff promises to respond to questions within 24 hours. Whether you are manning a phone or email hotline, be prepared for all kinds of questions. Don't be surprised if you can't answer all of them. Be honest. Simply say, "I'm sorry, but I'll need to consult with the writing center Director or another tutor. When can I get back to you?" or "I think you should talk with your instructor about that." It's better to admit lack of knowledge than to give students misinformation. Here is how Lori Salem, the writing center Director at Temple University, describes their hotline: "The questions run the gamut. Some students ask about a specific assignment. Others ask: 'Have I organized and expressed myself well?' Others ask for help in catching errors and proofreading" (Valenza).

In the Writing Fellows program at La Salle, the tutors initiated telephone conferencing on their own. Writing Fellows who are assigned to courses in the School of Nursing can rarely meet with the tutees. When we first began working with these courses, the Writing Fellows were not required to meet with the nursing students, but to respond in writing and return the papers to the students by giving them to the instructor for distribution. When Cynthia Finley Barry (the adult learner tutor introduced in Chapter 2) became a Writing Fellow, she suggested that the nursing students call her if they had questions. Cynthia, formerly a copy editor, was accustomed to discussing manuscripts by phone. Many of the nursing students were delighted to call her, and since then we have offered that option. Now the instructor collects the drafts, hands them over to the Writing Fellow, who reads them and writes comments. The drafts are then returned to the students who may call for a telephone conference. Janice Beitz, the nursing instructor you met in Chapter 5, has worked Writing Fellows for more than 10 years. Janice believes that this system is extremely effective. She says, "This is a wonderful program. Busy students really appreciate the chance to talk with the tutor as well as receive comments."

If you are a writing center tutor, and you want to try phone conferencing, students can submit their papers electronically and also arrange a time to talk by telephone. The Director of La Salle's writing center, Mary Robertson, uses a combination of online submission and telephone conferencing. Dr. Robertson believes that the telephone is not only a more effective way of responding to a draft than responding online, but that it's also more efficient. She says that she would spend more time formulating her ideas if she were writing comments, because she would be more concerned about clarity than when conferencing over the phone with the student's paper in hand.

Using Online Resources

Many writing centers have a variety of online resources (what we used to call "hand-outs") on their own OWL (Online Writing Lab) web page and also include links to OWL websites at other schools as well. You can use these sites during the tutoring process or tell students how to find them. OWL hand-outs are specifically designed explanations and examples of common writing problems and possible solutions or strategies to overcome them (McAndrew and Reigstad 124). You might be thinking, "But isn't all that information in writing handbooks?" Yes, indeed it is, but nowadays students may be more apt to use online resources than their freshman composition handbook, especially if they have already sold it back to the bookstore! Even if they own a hand-book, the students may be more apt to click on to the hand-out, which is directly related to their problem, rather than thumb through the handbook. Online information is available on virtually all topics related to writing. Here are two websites that are two of the La Salle tutors' "top picks" for students having trouble organizing their thoughts:

1. Purdue University, http://Purdue.edu/handouts/general/index. html
2. Linn Benton Community College Learning Center, http://cf. linnbenton.edu/depts/lrc/web.cfm?pgID=360.

For the student who can never remember where to find information about documentation (for example APA, MLA), the Online Style Guides may be the quickest way to solve that problem. The La Salle OWL has a link to the online Style Guides on our library's website.

Become familiar with the hand-outs on your school's OWL if you have one, or review some of the hand-outs on the OWL websites developed by other schools. Although most OWLs have similar hand-outs, the resources on a particular topic at one school may be especially effective. When in doubt, go to Purdue University's OWL: It boasts 130 hand-outs!

More About OWL Websites

The Writing Lab Newsletter features a monthly column of "What's New and/or Interesting on your Website." For example, the November 2003 issue featured The University of Wisconsin-Madison's writing center Website. Brad Hughes, director of their writing center, writes that "The OWL at the University of Wisconsin recently debuted a new structure and design for its online writing handbook." Hughes explains that the redesign is an attempt to organize reference materials based on how students use them. He cites research that indicates that "most people don't read deeply online, but want to obtain the information quickly by skimming." As a result, he and Les Howles, an instructional design specialist, developed "just in time" training materials, apparently to rave reviews from their students. Brad welcomes comments about this approach. See their website <http://www.wisc.edu/writing>. Most schools permit students from other schools to use their hand-outs, but they do have restrictions on the number that can be printed.

In addition to the hand-outs for students, many OWLs include resources for tutors such as tutoring tips and links to journals such as the *Writing Lab Newsletter* and the *Writing Center Journal*.

The Pitfalls of Online Tutoring: How to Avoid Them

The Last Minute Student

> My second round, which involved online tutoring, was not as enjoyable as the first, though this is not to say it was unenjoyable. It was initially complicated by the fact that some people were turning papers in late. I accepted a few late papers, but drew the line when people sent me their papers one or two days before the final draft due date.

Ryan Hoffmaster, the Writing Fellow quoted earlier in the chapter, refers to one of the frustrations a peer tutor faces—the last minute student. This problem may be even greater in the online context, because the student can type and send the draft without giving much thought to it. At the least, if the student is meeting you at the writing center, he needs to build in some time for an appointment, and he may use some of this time to review his draft or at least give some additional thought to this paper before meeting you.

Most writing centers and Writing Fellows Programs have strict guide-lines for submitting papers for review. Be sure that you are familiar with them and don't permit violations. If you are working in a peer-tutoring environment where the guidelines for submitting papers do not exist, or perhaps need to be revised, offer the writing center director some help. "The Boston College Online Writing Lab Guidelines" provide a good model:

> Any submissions received during regular OWL business hours will typically generate responses within 48 hours. Writers submitting during peak business periods (e.g. midterms, the end of the semester, etc.) may experience a wait time of as much as 72 hours. Tagging your submissions with time-sensitive headings such as urgent or ASAP or due tomorrow will not expedite the process or generate special priority handling. Always be sure to budget at least a three day turnaround window between the date of submission and the assignment due date.

Students are more apt to submit their drafts on time in Writing Fellows Programs if the instructor collects the drafts himself and then turns them over you. We encourage teachers participating in our Writing Fellows program to follow this procedure.

If you are a Writing Fellow and would like to try online tutoring, the submission requirements will be somewhat different than those appro-priate for writing centers. Because a Writing Fellow receives many drafts during a short time period (Writing Fellows at La Salle typically receive 10–15 drafts at once and have a week to return them to students), the submission guidelines must specify the date the drafts are due. You can see the potential problem: All the students could decide to submit their drafts on the last possible day.

The Invisible Assignment

I call the next problem, the "invisible assignment." You receive a paper or a question online, but no information about the assignment itself. Writing center tutors can ask students about the writing assignment when they see the students face to face, even if they don't bring a copy to the conference. Writing Fellows usually have a copy of the assignment from the instructor, but what about the tutor who receives a cyberspace draft? One possible solution: Construct a form for submitting papers that includes questions about the assignment.

The Invisible Student

"Personally I prefer the in-person conferences because they bring the tutor and the tutee on the same page." Once again we turn to Ryan's comments about his online tutoring experience. His attitude toward online tutoring is typical of many writing tutors who do their work this way. They miss the feedback they receive during the one-on-one conference. Gillespie and Lerner confirm our own observations at La Salle: "One of the most frustrating things for tutors can be the thundering silence that follows an e-response to a paper. After the face to face session, the writer is likely to let us know that we were helpful." But that's usually not the case with the online client (145).

You can try to get some feedback from the students you help online with a follow-up email, but don't be surprised if there is no response. Students are busy people, as you know. Their last writing assignment may be past history at the point they receive your follow-up email. Writing Fellows usually receive feedback through student surveys. At La Salle, the students in Writing Fellows–assisted courses complete an in-class survey. Most of these surveys are returned because students complete them in class. Writing Fellows are invited to review the surveys (which are anonymous) at the beginning of the following semester. Unfortunately online student surveys often don't elicit a high rate of return, according to Michael Rozkowski, the Director of Institutional Research at La Salle.

Conclusion

I love email. Like many American families, ours is in constant geographic flux. As I write this book, my younger brother is bracing himself for another freezing winter in Montreal, my older brother is sweltering in Dallas, and my sister-in-law is living in climatic bliss in Los Angeles. Before email, we may have phoned each other once every two or three months, sometimes even less frequently. Now we "talk" via email at least once or twice a week and share jokes even more often than that. Are all these emails quality conversations? Well, perhaps not. But cumulatively, these often hastily written messages have brought us closer together. At the risk of being accused of arguing by false analogy, I want to suggest that electronic conferencing has the potential of increasing the contact hours between tutors and students. The Director of the Writing Lab at Temple University reported that "the service is growing in popularity and the volume of questions is building. We saw 250 uses from October to mid-December" (Valenza). Perhaps some students who are willing to ask three or four questions using email (even at different stages of writing a paper) may not be willing or able to come to the writing center.

Don't get me wrong. Online tutoring will never replace the personal conference, just as email will never replace family visits. But as a peer tutor you should try it if you have the opportunity. Keep records of your experiences tutoring online, so you can compare online tutoring to conventional in-person tutoring; you can help us discover the full potential of this relatively new mode of helping students with their writing.

Questions for Discussion and Writing

1. Write an online response to the essay at the end of Chapter 6 (moral inquiry). Write an end comment and use the "Comment Function" to write comments in the margin. Compare your response to the checklist response to the paper.
2. Write an online response to the "Accidental Tourist" paper (end of Chapter 5). Compare your response online to your approach when responding at a conference.
3. Prepare a short annotated bibliography on the topic "Electronic Conferencing: What's New?" Read five essays written during the last year that appeared in one of the composition journals listed in "For Further Reading" of this chapter.
4. Write a persuasive essay about a controversial issue on your campus. Exchange essays with another peer tutor and comment online to each other's essay.
5. Review the resources on five OWL websites. Write a paragraph about the strengths and weaknesses of each.

Works Cited

Cooper, George, Karen Bui and Linda Riker. "Protocols and Process in Online Tutoring." *A Tutor's Guide: Helping Writers One to One.* Ed. Ben Raforth. Portsmouth, NH: Boynton/Cook Publishers, 2000.

Davis, Amy, Jackie Demedio and Jessica Greathouse. "Students Use of Online Resources: Educational Indexes Versus Common Search Engines." Paper written for English 360: Writing and the University, December 11, 2003, La Salle University.

Gillespie, Paula and Neal Lerner. *The Allyn and Bacon Guide to Peer Tutoring.* 1st ed. Needham Heights, MA: Allyn and Bacon, 2000.

Hoffmaster, Ryan. "Online Tutoring: A Report" Paper written for English 360: Writing and the University, December, 2002. Philadelphia, PA: La Salle University.

Honeycutt, Lee. "Comparing E-Mail and Synchronous Conferencing in Online Response." *Written Communication* 18:1 (January, 2001): 26–60.

Kastman-Breuch, Lee Ann, Merry, Rendahl and Michelle, Panuccio. "How Online Tutoring Matters: Benefits of Technology for Students and Tutors." Presentation, Conference on College Composition and Communication, Annual Conference, San Antonio, March, 2004.

Kuriloff, Peshe. "Redesigning Writing Instruction: How Technology Might Change the Writing Curriculum." Report to the Mellon Foundation, Philadelphia, PA: University of Pennsylvania, September, 2003.

McAndrew, Donald and Thomas Reigstad. *Tutoring Writing: A Practical Guide for Conferences.* Portsmouth, NH: Boynton/Cook Publishers, 2001.

Meyers, Emily and Louise Smith. *The Practical Tutor.* Oxford: Oxford University Press, 1987.

Monroe, Barbara. "The Look and Feel of the OWL Conference." *Wiring the Writing Center.* Ed. Eric Hobson, Logan, UT: Utah State University Press, 1998: 3–24.

Mullin, Joan A. "Writing Centers and WAC." *WAC for the New Millenium.* Ed. Susan McLeod, Eric Miraglia, Margot Soven, Christopher Thaiss. Urbana, IL: NCTE, 2001.

OWL: Online Tutoring Policies and Resources, Purdue University, *http://owl.purdue.edu/lab/owl/tutoring index.html.*

OWL: Online Writing Lab, Boston College, *http://www.bc.edu/libraries/centers/adc/online/*

Robertson, Mary. Director of the La Salle University Writing Center. Conversation, July, 2004.

Valenza, Joyce Kasman. "Writing Labs Reaching Out Online." *The Philadelphia Inquirer.* Thursday, March 2, 2000.

For Further Reading

Coogan, Dave. "E-Mail Tutoring: A New Way to Do New Work." *Computers and Composition* 12:2 (1995): 171–181.

Hawisher, Gail E. and Cynthia L. Selfe, Ed. *Passions, Pedagogies, and 21st Century Technologies.* Logan, UT: Utah State University Press and NCTE, 1999.

Hult, Christine and Joyce Kinkead, Ed. *Writing Centers Online.* A Special Issue of *Computers and Composition* 12:2 (1995).

Leigh, Ryan. *The Bedford Guide for Writing Tutors.* 3rd ed. Boston: Bedford St. Martins, 2002.

Spooner, Michael and Kathleen Yancy. "Postings on a Genre of Email." *College Composition and Communication* 47:2 (May, 1996): 252–278.

Index